CW01082018

JOAN DAVIES

Memories, Musings & More...

My Autobiography

JOAN DAVIES

Memories, Musings & More...

My Autobiography

Edited & Compiled by Louise Cook Edwards

IWriteYourStory.com

Dedication

Oh Gerry, How Much I Miss You!

My life is empty without you. We were always together, always out and about and finding a good story and just meeting people from all walks of life. As soon as the papers were in print, we delivered them, up to the mountains, the shopping areas, the seaside resorts, or the towns. Sometimes it was just one newspaper, but we made sure that everyone, but everyone, had a copy. It was interesting, invigorating, stimulating; it was a pleasure and we enjoyed the challenge. It was part of our lives.

After Gerry died I was lost. There was nothing more to live for.

After a few days, I shook myself. "Get on with it girl!" I said. Gerry would not like me grieving. So I did get on with it.

My book is ready. Enjoy it!

To Alan & Suzanne
Very Happy Memories to you both

Joan Davies

Joan Davies

Acknowledgements

Having started to write this book several years ago, I seriously doubted that it would ever see the light of day.

I would like to extend a big thank you to Louise Cook Edwards www.iwriteyourstory.com for making sense of my notes, filling in the gaps, collating all the material and bringing my whole story to life, and to Gary Edwards for taking my portraits, sifting through endless boxes of old photos and preparing the layouts.

Also to my former colleagues at *SUR in English*: Thank you to Liz Parry, Pedro Luis Gomez and Rachel Haynes for your kind words and support. We had such a lot of good times together!

Warm thanks also to my good friends Jesper Sander Pederson (President of the Costa Press Club), Jack Nusbaum, Nessie Wood, Wyn Calvin MBE, Elenna O'Harry, Peter Roberts, Genith Jones, Delyth Bressington, George Philip of Welsh Roots.

And to Bill Oliver, thank you so much for your invaluable advice and support.

With love,

Joan

JOAN DAVIES
Memories, Musings & More...

1st edition November 2013

Text Copyright © Joan Davies 2013

Edited & compiled by Louise Cook Edwards

Published by www.iwriteyourstory.com

Cover design & portrait © Gary Edwards

All photos courtesy of the author, with the exception of those supplied
by kind permission of *Diario SUR*, *SUR in English*, Gary Edwards,
Max Hilmar Hvid-Hansen, Bodegas Gongora SA, Marbella Club Hotel,
Suzan Davenport, Adrian Bracken, Costa Press Club, Wyn Calvin MBE.

ISBN 978-0-9927600-0-7

Contents

Dedication   5

Acknowledgements   7

Foreword - by Liz Parry   13

Timeline   15

Joan Davies - An Insight   17

Letters to Joan   21

Part 1: The Early Days

My Happy Childhood in Wales   29

We Called Her 'Mother'   31

Sister Brenda's Poem   33

School Days   37

Elenna Remembers   38

The Grandmother I Adored   42

Part 2: Joan Meets Gerry

Married in Five Days   49

All About Gerry   52

London or Paris, Perhaps?   52

The Big Move to Spain   55

Part 3: A New Life in Spain

The Journey South   59

Hello 60s Spain   63

Gerry Does What He Knows Best   64

An Encounter with El Generalísimo   65

Selling Wine for the Spaniards   67

Roasting on the Beach   68

The Good Life with Gerry   69

Part 4: The *SUR in English* Years

A Good Idea Waiting to Happen   73

The Once a Week Colleagues - by Pedro Luis Gomez   75

The Friday Couple - by Nigel Bowden   79

On the Cocktail Party Circuit with Joan and Gerry - by Jack Nusbaum   81

The Heart and Soul of *SUR in English* - by Louise Cook Edwards   85

Facts and Faces - Rubbing Shoulders with Celebs   90

SUR in English - Happy 15 Year Anniversary   103

Goodbye Dear Gerry   105

Part 5: My Musings on Life

The Sounds of Spain   109

Join the Club; Expat Life   111

A Romantic Train Ride   113

Falling for Marbella's Charms   115

Feasting in Andalusia   117

International Cuisine   119

Garlic Galore   120

The Chocolate Craze   120

Man About the Kitchen   121

Part 6: Life on My Own

Going It Alone   125

Downsizing My Life   125

My Mornings   130

Broken Confidence   130

Joining the Costa Press Posse   135

Honouring My Welsh Roots   141

In Fine Welsh Voice - The South Wales Male Choir   142

Wyn Calvin MBE - The Welsh Prince of Laughter   142

Haughty Portmeirion   144

Part 7: Joan's Travelogue

A Trip of a Lifetime   149

The Wonders of Sydney   149

The Great Barrier Reef   150

Cairns to Kuranda   151

The Fresh Taste of New Zealand   153

Meeting Cousin Iona   155

Our Whistle-Stop US Tour   157

Two Ladies in Las Vegas   157

Chicago is for Shopping   158

Pier 39, San Francisco   159

East Side Story; Warsaw and Cracow   161

Home - A Poem by Joan Davies and Bobby Kerrera   163

Foreword

When I think about Joan Davies, my mind goes straight back to the mid 80s when I first met two people who were going to change my life. Joan and Gerry Davies were living in Calahonda, in the epicentre of what was fast becoming the expat residential area *par excellence* and had seen an opening, a *need,* for a newspaper in English. I was living in Malaga, home to the local Spanish newspaper, and was ready to return to work now that my babies were safely in nursery school.

What happened next forms part of this book, but is by no means the beginning or the end of it. In the years we worked together, meeting once a week at the *SUR* offices in Malaga, I got to know a lot more of Joan's story. She would arrive with her typewriter and settle in to the newsroom, bringing with her tales of celebrities, the Marbella 'jet-set' was the term we used, chief ministers, top sports people, and others who were changing the area from a series of fishing villages into the major tourist destination it is now. Joan knew everyone. She and Gerry rubbed shoulders with all the movers and shakers of the Costa del Sol, and took photos of them to be developed in the Malaga offices of *SUR* and inserted into the pages of their brainchild.

And of course, it wasn't only work we talked about. Joan and Gerry were true pioneers of the foreign resident phenomenon and had experimented with other ventures on the Costa del Sol until the expat community grew big enough to support a weekly English language newspaper. I heard about their earlier life in Wales and their whirlwind romance. We talked a lot about food - when she wasn't working or out socializing, I got the impression that Joan spent her time baking the most delicious cakes - and for many years she made use of her culinary expertise to write the 'Food for Thought' page in *SUR in English.*

It wasn't long before other foreign language media joined *SUR in English* in serving the expat population, and Joan's pioneering spirit came to the fore again. "We need to share our experiences," she would say to me. "I think we should have an association". And now, thanks to Joan and her contacts, we have a flourishing Costa Press Club.

If it hadn't been for Joan, *SUR in English* would not have hit the streets on 20th July 1984. Nor would it have become the almost overnight success that it was, requiring more people to work on it. And if it hadn't been for Joan telling the Spanish management of *SUR* that I was the right candidate for an editorial post in Malaga, I wouldn't be where I am now. The coast would be a different place if Joan and Gerry had never decided to uproot themselves and come here, and my life would not have been the same either.

Writing a foreword to Joan's story has been a pleasure. On behalf of myself and many other people whose lives she has touched, I'd like to say, "Thank you Joan".

Liz Parry

Editor - *SUR in English*

JOAN DAVIES

Timeline

22nd November 1929 Elizabeth Diane Joan Hughes was born in Coventry.

1932 The Hughes family moved to Pwllheli, Wales.

1935 The family moved to Ellesmere, Shropshire. Joan went back and forth between there and Pwllheli, Wales, regularly staying with her grandparents. She would visit great grand parents in Welshpool.

1935 Attended Troedyrallt Infant School and Primary School followed by the County School in Pwllheli.

1948 Joan attended Bangor College to qualify as a teacher.

1951 Joan took a teaching job in Moss Side, Manchester followed by another teaching position in Cheadle Hulme.

1955 During the Easter holidays, whilst in Wales, Joan met Gerry Davies.

1st April 1955 Joan married Gerry after a whirlwind courtship. The couple lived for a time in Llanarthney with Gerry's family.

1955 Gerry secured a job with the *Daily Mail* and the couple moved briefly to London. They lived briefly in Paris when Gerry worked for an American newspaper group.

1961 Gerry's father fell ill and died of cancer and Joan and Gerry returned to Wales to run the family business for a while.

1964 Joan and Gerry sold the family business and emigrated to Spain, living in a fisherman's cottage in Los Boliches on the Costa del Sol, Malaga.

1966 Gerry worked for the *Daily Mail*, travelling all over Spain as a distribution manager. The couple lived briefly in Madrid before settling definitively on the Costa del Sol on the south coast. Joan contributed to the *Daily Mail* and was accredited by the International Press Association.

1970s Joan and Gerry ran a beach restaurant, Las Banderas, in Marbella and two bars in Mijas Costa.

20th July 1984 Joan and Gerry Davies co-founded *SUR in English* with Prensa Malagueña. The first edition was 16 pages. A runaway success story, in 2014, the newspaper celebrates its 30th anniversary. The couple were the heart and soul of the paper, compiling the stories and selling advertising as well as covering the thriving expat social scene.

8th June 1995 Gerry Davies died. For the first and only time, the *SUR in English* shouted "Stop Press!" in order to reprint the paper featuring a tribute to Gerry from his bereaved colleagues which appeared the following day in the 9th June edition.

2002 Joan and her sister Lowrie took an extended trip to Australia to visit a cousin and enjoyed exploring Australia, New Zealand as well as several American towns.

2002 Joan founded Welsh Roots, a social club gathering together Welsh residents and visitors on the Costa del Sol.

May 2004 Joan was a founder member of the Costa Press Club and was made Honorary President that year.

2007 Until this year, Joan continued to write for *SUR in English*, attending events for her 'Facts and Faces' column and cooking up recipes for 'Food for Thought'.

2013 Joan publishes her memoirs, JOAN DAVIES, *Memories, Musings & More...* with the assistance of Louise Cook Edwards. www.iwriteyourstory.com

JOAN DAVIES

An Insight

September 2013

I consider myself an ordinary person who has done some extraordinary things. I get on with life. I am a happy person and don't dwell on problems. I think that is a lot to do with my upbringing. When there are nine children, you are not given the luxury of obsessing over trivia. I love writing and meeting people, and this was key to my life as a teacher, and then as a journalist. I appreciate people who are honest and kind.

What is the most important thing in your life?
My friends and family.

Who in your life would you thank?
I think you have to thank everyone all the time - it's a small word that means a lot. My siblings and I owe a lot to our grandparents. They taught us what was right and wrong.

What is the hardest thing you have had to do in your life?
Being parted from the people I love.

Any guiding principles in your life?
You have to give as well as take, and be nice to people.

And the important lessons?
Learning from my grandparents - they were strict but caring and taught us to find our strengths and limitations.

If you only had one day left to live, how would you spend it?
Find a good friend and spend the day drinking a Magnum of champagne! I'd bequeath everything I've got to my sister Brenda - she can share it with rest of the family.

How would you best like to be remembered?
As a person who has enjoyed life, and who has not done anything wrong - certainly not intentionally - and as a person who has been loved.

How would you describe yourself as a child?
I was a bit spoiled. I liked getting my own way. I was the eldest, always happy and always the leader; captain of the netball and hockey teams, mad on sport.

What's the best job you ever had?
Starting and working for *SUR in English*. It opened up so many possibilities.

Worst job?
My first teaching job - it was in a rough school in Manchester. I couldn't cope with the things going on, even in those days.

What can you not live without?
Appreciation.

Is there anything you would change about yourself?
No, I'm quite happy as I am.

If there were a fire in your house, what possessions would you save?
There was actually a fire in my apartment complex once, luckily only a small one. I went back for my handbag!

If you could meet anyone in the world, who would it be?
Nelson Mandela. He's a true man of the people, who personifies kindness and compassion.

Did you ever want children?
We were such a big family, it didn't really cross my mind.

What does love mean to you?
Kindness.

What are your best qualities?
Honesty and gratitude.

And your worst points?
I can't be a Saint?

What are the advantages of getting older?
Not many!

What do you like best about your home?
Having someone to do the housework and overlooking the pool - I love to be able to see the water.

Do you believe in God?
I've got no religious yearnings but I believe in God. Sometimes I wonder what He's doing? I don't believe in an afterlife. Occasionally, I go to church with friends on a Sunday and quite enjoy it - but I tend not to go regularly to anything.

Is there anything you would still like to accomplish?
Celebrating getting this book out! I have been writing it on and off for years. I thought it would be easy, and now I feel as though I have accomplished a long treasured goal.

L.C.E.

Wyn Calvin MBE, Entertainer on Joan Davies

For over twenty-five years our visits to the Costa del Sol have been highlighted by meetings with Pwllheli's answer to good communication and fine cuisine; Joan Davies.

Many British residents in southern Spain will be aware of Joan's recipes and her chatty columns in *SUR in English* - but only a few of us have had the privilege of actually enjoying Joan's famous meals in her own home. I must say they were delightful, delicious and memorable. There has also been the joy of conversations in which Joan would bring us up-to-date with news and views of folk and frolics on the Costa... Who said the Welsh don't gossip?

Over the years, Joan has supported and shown great interest in various charities in the area. All who know her - and those that knew Gerry too - will be aware of their valuable contribution to the life of British and English-speaking expats in this special region of Spain with the newspaper they founded and their involvement in many groups.

Now we will know a bit more about Joan...

With best wishes,

Wyn

Jack Nusbaum,
Friend & Fellow Journalist
on Joan Davies

In the 80s I began to meet up with Joan and Gerry regularly at press events. Spanish was a bit of a problem for the Davies, but I knew a little. Joan hooked on to me for help, "Jack, who is he?" or "What was he saying?" or "Can you introduce me?"

Gerry always seemed to have time to kill at these events and, as a wine connoisseur would enjoy a tasting session. There would invariably be various *tapas* passed around by roving waiters, and Gerry, of course, loved nibbling as he sipped.

With a press pack in her hand, Joan would quiz me about the info, her ballpoint pen and notepad flying at high speed. Her articles would appear in the appropriate sections of *SUR in English* a week or two later, and heaps of praise were usually sent to Joan for the splendid job she did.

Joan carried on writing for *SUR in English* until only a few years ago when retirement time came around. She remains very active with all kinds of personal projects. And as part of the establishment of the Costa Press Club, since helping to found it in 2004, attending the monthly meetings has been really pleasurable for Joan, helping to keep her constantly busy and productive.

Who said Joan is retired!

Jack

A Letter to Joan Davies
from Christine Shaw 1998

Several weeks ago, I received a newsletter from Christine Shaw, a great and wonderful friend who owned a prestigious Beauty Academy in Estepona.

She thanked me profusely and was touched by my concern. She had gone through a difficult time and was slowly getting back to normality. She included a special note to me, addressed to:

SUR in English founder, Joan Davies, stating that I had been a pillar of strength to her at the time.

Thank you Christine. I quote the letter:

"Life is a challenge - Need it

Life is tense - Ease it

Life is a promise - Keep it

Life is tough - Smooth it

Life is a duty - Do it

Life is life - Live it!"

Such true words...

I wiped away a few tears and carried on with her letter. I was so touched.

PART 1

The Early Days

My Happy Childhood in Wales

I was born on 22nd November 1929, Elizabeth Diane Joan Hughes, in Coventry, the daughter of John Trevor and Claire Olive Hughes. But while I was still a baby, my parents returned to North Wales, to a small town called Pwllheli, on the Lleyn Peninsula where my grandparents lived. As far as I'm concerned, I'm Welsh through and through. My father John Trevor Hughes worked in the bank in Pwllheli and we moved in to live with my grandparents.

My mother was very young when I was born, just 17; I was her first so she was glad of the help my grandmother was able to provide. My father came from the island of Anglesey on the Menai Straits. His family owned a prosperous painting and decorating emporium in the High Street of Menai Bridge. In no time at all, another baby was on the way, and shortly afterwards, my father was moved to Ellesmere in Shropshire. It was a pretty, rather quaint village alongside a large mere and was popular with tourists from the Midlands.

The family settled down there and continued to grow. Inevitably, when another baby came along, my grandmother offered to take me for a couple of weeks to help my mother out. I recall staying with her one lovely summer; I had a wonderful time, playing on the beach, swimming and fishing with the other children.

Grandmother was fabulous, and I enjoyed myself so much that I wanted to live with her, so she let me stay long-term and I went to the local school in Pwllheli. Living with my grandparents, Elizabeth and Jack Davies was wonderful; they were the happiest days of my life; I was loved and spoiled. My grandparents were the kindest and gentlest of people and I adored them, but my grandmother was also strict; she was tall and stately with a strong character.

Right: The family home owned by my parents, John Trevor and Claire Olive Hughes, Rhosimere, Elson, Ellesmere.

Below: The complete Hughes family line up, taken in 1956. Ken, Jenny, Brenda, my Mother Claire Olive, Alun, my father John Trevor, me, Lowrie, Johnny, Sian and Janet.

We Called her "Mother"

Elizabeth was born in the historic town of Welshpool as Elizabeth Vansoist, and my grandfather Jack was a railway man. I loved getting on the train with my grandmother when she went to see the family. She was always immaculately dressed, down to her fur stole or tippet.

My grandmother Elizabeth's brothers lived in Welshpool, on the Welsh border next to Shropshire, and there were always kisses and hugs all round. I remember when I was about 12 years old, sitting in the middle of a large table of aunts and uncles, cousins, etc. I didn't say a word. There wasn't a chance, and I liked it that way.

I noticed how well turned out everyone was. They were a family of tailors; my uncle was tailor to the Marquis of Anglesey. One of the things that grandmother always insisted upon was that we attended Sunday school every week. She brought us up to be honest and independent. She came from a large family and taught us that we had to go our own way and become individuals, with our own thoughts and ideas.

We called our grandmother "Mother"; she was the one who held the family together. I was the eldest of nine children, six girls and three boys. My brother Alun attended the Royal College of Art & Design and became a successful fashion designer in London during the 60s with clients such as Diana Rigg. Sian married a wealthy man and bought a boutique. Brother Kenneth joined the RAF and enjoyed the life so much, he made it his career. Sisters Lowrie and Jennifer both married and had families. Another sister Janet moved to Australia. Then there is Johnny, the youngest and my sister, Brenda is the closest in age after me. We all had a wonderful childhood thanks to my grandparents.

Brenda was two years younger than me. She was a very pretty girl and, I have to admit, she was a bit of a flirt! By the time we were in our teens, the Second World War had broken out, and there were lots of service men stationed in the area. Brenda and I used to walk to school together, in our school uniforms, and we would pass the soldiers and sailors as they marched the six miles to the multi-services camp on the outskirts of Pwllheli. There was an American base too, and many of the local girls ended up marrying soldiers. Brenda loved to wave at the soldiers, while I would hide behind her!

I liked school and passed the scholarship exam to attend the County School, which was at the top of the hill in Pwllheli. It was a good school and I got on well there. The headmistress, Miss Price, a ferocious looking woman, was a force unto herself. She ruled with a rod of iron, but we loved and respected her.

Afterwards, I attended Bangor College; it was situated in a lovely building, alongside the University, with a glorious view of the Menai Straits and its graceful, elegant bridges. It was a delight to study there. I qualified as a teacher.

I remember what it was like growing up during the War, although in many ways we didn't feel like there was a War on in Wales; the bombing was at a distance. When I was staying in Welshpool there were some air raids. The family had gone to the pub and I was looking after the little ones. I heard bombs; they were over Liverpool. We all huddled up together waiting for them to pass. It was petrifying. We lived in an end house, right next to a lovely farm. As my grandmother knew the farmer, we had all the perks including fresh butter and eggs and were therefore relatively unaffected by all the rationing.

My father was in the RAF during the War, stationed in India for four long years. As happened all too often with wartime marriages, my mother had a boyfriend, an American officer and my father had a lady friend in India.

The Americans had silk stockings and chocolates to woo the ladies. I remember mother's boyfriend. He struck me as too smooth, and he seemed to come around too often... But the women had a good time with the Americans. After the War, my father came home and simply slotted back into the swing of family life. My parents had both had a fling and afterwards there was no remorse, they simply got on with things.

My mother, Claire Olive Hughes was born in 1912. She was exceptionally pretty. When she was just 13, she was chosen to be 'May Queen' of Pwllheli. This was a great honour, and her parents were most proud with her being their only daughter. As 'Queen' she was showered with gifts; a gold watch, numerous items of jewellery, and other trinkets, offered by the town's big wigs. What a day it must have been!

Lloyd George who became Prime Minister from 1916-1922 was Welsh and his family had a home in the vicinity. He was a most impressive statesman, with a long mass of grey hair and known to be a notorious womanizer. Everyone would sing, "Lloyd George knew my father, My father knew Lloyd George." And we children would add, "Perhaps he knew my mother too!"

Brenda's Family Tree

At the head of Brenda's family

sits Lady Olive Claire.

A lady of distinction

no other can compare.

Then out in Spain is sister Joan

soaking up the sun.

She says that going over there

was the best thing she's ever done.

The oldest son is Kenneth

The RAF has been his life,

but now he has retired

to the country with his wife.

Next is daughter Jenny

the girl without a care.

She's well set up in Chester

married to a millionaire.

Then we come to Alun

the joker of the pack.

He lives in a tiny cottage

well off the beaten track.

Let's not forget dear sister Sian

in her shop of well renown.

She sells the highest fashions,

it's the Harrods of her town.

Then we come to Johnny

the youngest of the brood.

Another Arthur Daley,

but he'd help you if he could.

Next we come to Janet

the artist of the clan.

She's living in Australia

painting pictures oh so grand.

So now we come to Lowrie

Joan Collins of the team.

She's married to a copper

and very happy it would seem.

At last we come to Brenda

gentle, sweet and kind.

No matter where you travel

no better you could find.

-- o --

Above: A painting of the view from the County School looking down onto Pwllheli.

Below: With a holiday friend Alwen and siblings, Alun and Brenda. c.1949.

Above: 6th Form at Grammar School in Pwllheli. I'm sitting second from the left with Elenna on my right.

Below: Troedyralt Infants School in Pwllheli, aged 5, I'm in the second row, second from the left, again with Elenna on my right.

School Days

I attended Troedyrallt Primary School. My best friend was Elenna Hughes. We were always together, winter or summer, rain or shine, playing rounders or netball down on the beach.

At the tender age of 11, we both won scholarships for the County School. Wearing our dark green and yellow school uniforms, along with our leather satchels, together we walked proudly up to school at the top of the hill behind Pwllheli. As she was an only daughter, Elenna's mother was often in tow.

It was a happy time when we were forging our independence. We were given brand new bicycles, as was normal when you passed the scholarship and with our sweethearts, we paired off for picnics on the beach - it was wonderful! I had a boyfriend but we lost touch when I left for Bangor College. I enjoyed my time there. Even then, it was quite a cosmopolitan place, with students attending from all over the world. Elenna met a fellow student, Harry, from South Wales, and when they married, I was a bridesmaid.

We also lost touch for a while, but Elenna recently came back into my life. I was so pleased. She had a career as a conductor with an orchestra in Wales, travelling all over the world and teaching music. Someone mentioned her name and I said, "There can only be one Elenna O'Harry!" Then she called me - she was on holiday in Spain. We reminisced for hours about climbing up hills, playing games, and all the things we did as children and teenagers. After her holiday she wrote me the most wonderful letter full of insights into our early life together...

8th August 2013

Dear Joan,

I've been searching through old albums and diaries for anything that might be of interest to you! I quite enjoyed the task. It's much better than housework. Pre-war days are practically lost in the mists of time I'm afraid. I don't suppose we met before starting school and from then on, we were usually in a threesome with Dorothy Dale. I'm enclosing a photo taken with Miss Roberts, the headmistress in 1936. The infant's school building is due to be demolished to make room for housing. I served as a magistrate at court for several years, but all cases now go to Caenarfon. The church hall has also been pulled down and more houses will be built there as well.

As far as I remember we played most of our games out on the road. There was not much traffic in those days! I do remember though that your father Trevor had a car. That was very posh in those days! We played a lot of ball games like 'Tensies' and 'Porch'. Usually we played on the concrete in front of the Dickinson's garage. Other games I remember are, 'The Farmer Wants a Wife', 'Three Jolly Welshmen', 'Tici', and 'In and Out the Dusking Bluebells'. There must have been others.

In the summer, we spent most of our time on Abersoch Beach, making sand castles, digging holes to make little houses and playing hide and seek in the dunes. Of course, there were sand-covered sandwiches and lovely homemade ice-creams from Mrs. Jones's shop. Our lives changed with the outbreak of war in 1939. I started keeping a diary in 1940 and I've come across others for 1942 and 1946 and a later one for 1949. These are written in English, which seems very strange to me today as nowadays, I write my diaries in Welsh. The one from 1940 is very sparse and uninteresting, but I've had a lot of laughs reading the 1942 one! It isn't full by any means, but it certainly brings back memories!

I remember that we had been to the pictures to see a film starring Canadian born actress, Deanna Durbin, in which she was a member of a secret society at her school. This prompted us to start one of our own. We called it the Penguins Secret Society (P.S.S.) for short because our mascot was my soft toy called Peggy Penguin and because it was mine, I became Captain! The other members were, Joan Hughes, Superintendant, Dorothy Dale, Secretary, Era Roberts, Senior and J.H. Secretary, Haf Parry, Senior and Brenda Hughes, Junior. We had badges made of pop bottle stoppers! We signed a piece of paper in red ink and called it 'The Treaty'. It was put in a bottle and buried by our back gate. We had to salute it every time we passed!

We seem to have spent many evenings in the cinema. As my mother was working on the cash desk, we were allowed in for nothing!

You and I both had bicycles for passing our scholarship to the County School and we spent many a happy hour riding around the area. Later, we were joined by our boyfriends! I don't know what happened to Charlie or Peter Warrener, but David (E.B.) sadly passed away last year during a visit to his sister's home in Fflint.

The 1949 diary is an account of life in Bangor. We met there on a fairly regular basis for coffee and dances in Jimmy's (St. James's Church). We also often went home to Pwllheli on Sundays, getting a lift on the creamery lorries and catching the bus back. During the holidays we again spent a lot of time in the Palladium and the Youth Club (which by then we found rather boring). To go back to 1946, there is not much of interest in the diary, accounts of visits to the Palladium and of netball matches in school (now called a Grammar School). I also note that I had my first banana after the War!

In September, we had a new Headmaster, Mr. R.E. Hughes, father of Erye, Haf and Manon. Eryl's youngest daughter, Ffion was a member of Cor Godre's Eifl for several years, but died of ovarian cancer a couple of years ago at the age of 42. I miss her.

One or two things have now come back to me about the infant's school. I remember making calendars in Miss Griffith's class and learning to knit in Miss White's. When we were in her class, Ronnie Williams died of Meningitis, aged 7. His sister died before that, aged 4 of diptheria. I remember that they lived back to back with your house. Their mother was the sister of Beti Mai's mother.

I remember a few things about the big school, eg. singing lessons with Mr. Cook and then with Mr. Jones (Jo-Jo). Songs such as *Boney was a Warrior*, *The Maple Leaf*, or *Canada Round ye Horn*. Strange choices don't you think? We were taught to write instead of printing by Mrs. Jones Penlan Bach who used to slap our fingers with a ruler if we didn't hold the pen properly!

John Elfyn Roberts taught us pounds, shillings and pence and many's the time he sent me to the cloakroom for laughing. Guess who told me the jokes! We all liked Mr. Roberts but were scared of the Headmaster, Mr. Wheldon Hughes who was very handy with the use of his cane! Do you remember the school dentist, Mr. Parry? He filled a tooth for me once and slapped me for squealing! Happy days!

It was lovely to have a chat on the phone. Do keep in touch!

Love from,

Elenna O'Harry   xx

P.S.

I have enclosed a couple of recent things you might like to see! I've also remembered one or two more things.

Just after Dunkirk, a number of the soldiers who had been saved were brought to a camp near Yokehouse. You and I were walking past The Black Lion one day, when a couple of soldiers came out and gave us each a French coin. I still have that little centime piece - to think that it came to Pwllheli via Dunkirk! Did you keep yours?

Funny things come to mind don't they? If we saw a man with a white hat, we would chant, *Ht wen a ruban du - lwc I mi a pinsh I chi*! Another memory is of the two of us hiding under the table eating the remains of the birthday party food after all the others had gone home!

I remember that at one time you had a lovely little dog called Bonzo whom we used to tease. I think he was a terrier of sorts and was mainly white in colour. He nipped my leg once; I can't blame him!

The photos from the Cyniro were taken in 1939, two years before we went to the County School. I recognize the men on the staff but not the women on the right. From L to R the men are R.R. Jones, Bill Jenkins, Caradog Jones, T.H. Jones, R. Williams (whom we called Big Boy), Llewllyn Hughes, Ednyfed Jones, Rev. Theodore James, Mr. Hughes. The women are Averilda Williams, Daisy Glyn Jones and Miss Muriel Price. One of the ladies on the right must be Miss Williams, but I don't know which one. She later became Mrs. Jones-Pierce.

Must stop and get this to the post. If I find anything else, I will let you know. Most of my photos have been stuck in albums so are almost impossible to scan. I now realize my mistake! E.

Above: With Elenna Hughes in Pwllheli.

Left: Me on the right with Elenna and her husband Harry at their wedding in the 1950s.

The Grandmother I Adored

Somewhere in the town of Rochdale, Lancashire, in the year 1889, on a stormy night, a woman gave birth to a baby, a daughter whose name was to be Elizabeth Vansoist Davies, my grandmother. She was no ordinary woman and after an amazing life, finally died some 94 years later. We thought she was immortal because she would often say, "I'll live until my bones are dropping." She passed away peacefully, not in the dead of night, but reaching out to another day, and we were there with her.

During his working years, Elizabeth's father was a master tailor and true gentleman. As a man of importance around town, Mr. Davies would acknowledge everyone, tipping his hat with ease. His wife was a lady in the real meaning of the word. They lived in a fine house on top of the hill in the town of Welshpool, kept several working staff and it was in this house that Elizabeth spent her childhood. He was one of seven children, four of them ministers of religion, but I know little of his wife, my great grandmother. In later years, circumstances changed and he started to drink heavily. He became the 'black sheep' of the family and they moved into a smaller house in a narrow alleyway, and it was there I remember them living.

Elizabeth was of a rebellious nature. Wearing long ringlets, she would often roll her hair around her fingers, a trait which I inherited myself. She ran away from home several times, and at the tender age of 15, she went to a nearby infirmary to train as a nurse. The discipline was too much for her, and at 16 she ran away once again, this time to work in a tearoom in a small village station. It was here that she met her future husband Jack, a dashing young railwayman who all the girls used to chase. But once Elizabeth made up her mind and declared that he was for her, they were married in a Registry Office. There was no chapel for Elizabeth and Jack. Although her husband's family were deeply religious, she could not and would not tolerate their 'old-fashioned' ideas.

A newcomer appeared on the scene, her sister-in-law Jane, and there was a lot of ill feeling between the three of them. Jane had lost her husband in a coal-mining accident in South Wales. She was of no help to Elizabeth. In fact, she was more of a hindrance, attempting to get Elizabeth to attend the Chapel on a Sunday and Bible classes during the week. This was all too much for Elizabeth, and she acquired a taste for stout now and then, and Jane did not approve of that! So Elizabeth made her own way in life, taking in paying guests, always railwaymen, men from Porthmadoc, Machynlleth and the Barmouth area and men who were to become life-long friends. She had an eye for the men, always with a nod and a wink for a handsome chap! She and Jack lived in a modest terraced house with bay windows, outside which their future daughter, Claire Olive, would walk on a red carpet when she was elected 'May Queen'.

Above: My Mother, Claire Olive, the May Queen of Pwllheli in 1925.

Above and below: Treasured paintings made in the 1960s by local artist and friend, Gwlym Roberts of the sailing boat which Gerry and I owned in Pwllheli.

*To alun.
with love
Diana*

Above: Signed photograph of my brother Alun, fashion designer, with Diana Rigg in the 1960s.

PART 2

Joan Meets Gerry

Married in Five Days

After Bangor College, where I had completed my teacher training, I was sent to work in a school in Manchester. Sadly, my first job was in Moss Side senior school, and I hated it. Even in those days, it was a very rough area and some of the kids were unruly; they would clap their hands together and say things like, "Oh, look at her, she's got a new hat" or "Nice pair of trousers Miss!" (And much worse comments when I reacted of course). The boys were about 14 or 15 years old and I was only 21. I simply couldn't handle them. I just hated them and the school, so I left and went to another school in Cheadle Hulme, a more select area, which I loved! The school was pleasant and the children were well behaved. At the time, I had a couple of casual boyfriends, then a steady one called Charlie. I was quite fond of him, and thought, maybe this was 'it', but I knew there was something missing.

During the Easter break from school, I went back home and everything changed. I met Gerry and within five days we were married. Actually, we decided to marry after only three days, but getting the licence took longer.

I was taking my little brother Alun for a walk and a car kept coming alongside us and stopping. My brother said, "I think that fellow wants to talk to you." The car drove off and disappeared. We continued to walk, and then it reappeared. "He's here again." Alun said, but the car drove off.

The next day, Gerry returned and asked me to join him for a coffee. In the end, I succumbed, and with my brother in tow, we went to a cafe. I agreed to go out with him. Gerry was 22 at the time, charming and very handsome. I fell for him, hook, line and sinker and I had no doubt at all that it was the same for him. When he asked me to marry him, I immediately said, "Yes!"

Four days later, I announced to my parents, "We're getting married tomorrow, are you coming?" Naturally they were furious! Because of his work in the bank, my father couldn't come, and neither could my mother. Only Alun and Brenda were there; nobody from Gerry's family; they didn't want to know anything about us. They wished for him to marry a Welsh girl, and although my parents were Welsh, and I speak the language, as I was born in Coventry, they didn't consider me Welsh!

Gerry and I were married at Bangor Registry Office on 1st April 1955. My big concern was what should I wear for my wedding. I found a beautiful white and cream dress that looked lovely, and was suitable for the honeymoon too. Sadly, when I got back from our honeymoon, I took the dress to the cleaners and it got lost; I never saw it again. After we were married, we moved to Menai Bridge and lived on the Straits.

No. Rhif 69	Marriage solemnized at Priodas a weinyddwyd yn Register Office				in the district of yn nosbarth Bangor	in the yn County of Caernarvon	
1. When married Pryd y priodwyd	2. Name and surname Enw a chyfenw	3. Age Oed	4. Condition Cyflwr	5. Rank or profession Safle neu broffesiwn	6. Residence at the time of marriage Preswylfa adeg priodi	7. Father's name and surname Enw a chyfenw'r tad	8. Rank or profession of father Safle neu broffesiwn y tad
First April	Gerald Davies	22 years	Bachelor	Newspaper Representative	2 Deiniol Road Bangor	Geoffrey Thomas Davies	Post master
1955	Elizabeth Diana Joan Hughes	25 years	Spinster	Teacher	Glanmorva Beswick Road Pwllheli	John Trevor Hughes	Bank Clerk

Married in the Priodwyd yn Register Office				
This marriage was solemnized between us, Gwnaethpwyd y briodas hon rhyngom ni,	G. Davies	in the presence of us, yn ein presenoldeb ni,	W. Vizard	by licence before me, drwy gennyf fi, R Hughes Supt. Registrar
	J. Hughes		E. Vizard Superintendent	J Vaughan Jones Registrar

Certified to be a true copy of an entry in a register in my custody.
Tystiolaethwyd ei fod yn gopi cywir o gofnod mewn cofrestr a gedwir gennyf i. Gwendolie Thomas (Signature Llofnod)

Registration District Dosbarth Cofrestru Bangor

WARNING: A CERTIFICATE IS NOT EVIDENCE OF IDENTITY. RHYBUDD: NID YW TYSTYSGRIF YN PROFI PWY YDYCH CHI.

Above: Our Wedding Certificate 1st April 1955. April Fools Day - many a joke was made!

Opposite: Gerry and I pose for our wedding portrait.

All About Gerry

Gerry was born on 23rd May 1932 in South Wales. His family lived in Llanarthney, a small Welsh village. His father Goronwy, 'Gonny' was the Post-Master, and something of a 'bigwig' in the town. They were quite insular, and doted on Gerry. He was quite spoiled. He had a very pretty sister who died young. The officers from the American camp would use the family's shop and post office. She fell in love with one of them. Sadly, her father wouldn't let her marry him, which broke her heart. She died of cancer in her thirties.

Gerry attended a public school, Llandovery College, a famous rugby school. I don't think he learned much, but he did become quite a good 'rugger' player and after leaving school enjoyed watching as well as regularly playing. When we first met we went to every match. There was much revelry afterwards. They were a fabulous bunch of blokes and very charitable. Many of them were just starting their medical careers. The partners and wives would come along after the games; everyone would dress up and it was quite a party atmosphere. Invariably though, the men would drift off and get drunk.

Gerry loved sailing as well as rugby and we would sail all along the coast in our boat for most of the summer. Pwllheli has a lovely little harbour full of pleasure and fishing boats.

London or Paris, Perhaps?

Gerry was a newspaperman. He was a brilliant advertising salesman and worked in distribution too. First he was with the *Western Mail* in Swansea. Then was he was moved to Manchester. One day he came home and said that he had been offered a job in London with the *Daily Mail*. He was very excited, so we moved to London within days and I found another teaching job.

I can't say I warmed to life in the capital. We were living quite far out of town, our flat was rather dreary and although it was the 60s and Gerry had a job on a Fleet Street paper, life was not exactly 'swinging' for us. After not too long I was pleased when I learned the paper had decided to relocate Gerry to work in Paris... Paris! How wonderful!

We were very happy in Paris. I got another part-time job teaching English to French children and loved it! When we first arrived, our priority was to find somewhere to live. It was not as easy as we thought; prices were sky high, so we settled for a dwelling on the edge of town on Rue Sixième. Our apartment was not in the most salubrious of buildings. The lift was ancient, and the sound of it creaking up and down was quite horrendous.

I used to drive Gerry to his office on the Champs Elysees and back home each day. After dropping him and if I was not working, I would often take myself off to the banks of the Seine, sit in a café watching the world go by or take a picnic to one of the parks. The *Daily Mail* offices closed at three, so we made the most of our afternoons, often driving out into the countryside. I had my first taste of continental life and I absolutely adored it.

However early one afternoon in the centre of Paris, I found myself in the middle of a scuffle with the police... It was not very pleasant. I didn't realize how bad it was until I saw the water cannons. People were screaming in a language I hardly understood, and I found myself being pushed, shoved and lifted into one of the stores. The streets were overflowing, and there were police in wet gear all over the place. It was terrifying...

Then, suddenly the yelling and crying stopped and there was silence. The police had done their job and slowly but nervously crowds dispersed and the streets emptied. It was a horrific experience. I felt numb and disorientated, but managed to find the car and make for home. By the time I'd reached the apartment, I had calmed down. Gerry said, "Did you have a nice day, *cherie*?" I sat down and burst into tears.

We probably would have stayed longer in Paris, but Gerry's father died suddenly and we were needed at home. So, once again we found ourselves back in Wales in the tiny village of Llanarthney. Gerry was expected to take over the running of the business, which he did very well and I found a job in the local school, which was fine. However, the atmosphere in the home was icy. In the early days, Gerry's parents had always resented me, rarely talking to me and even at this time his mother, who admittedly had mellowed over the years, was still cold.

Gerry gave it a go for a while but eventually decided to sell the shop. The truth was that we both hated the village and the store. The business sold well, and as soon as we had the money in hand, we decided to leave. Gerry said, "So where do we go now?" Straight away, I said, "Spain!"

The Big Move to Spain

It was 1964, and we were leaving for Spain.

For a while we didn't tell my parents or Gerry's mother. But when they found out they all thought we were out of our minds and couldn't believe we were seriously planning to live abroad again. "Why?" They implored. "You've got a good job Gerry, and so has Joan". But life is like that, and we did not mention it further. "Leave it alone for a while," I said to Gerry.

We wanted to tell the world we were leaving. I can't keep a secret for long, so when the time actually came, we surreptitiously put some of our belongings in a large suitcase. I have never been a person who could travel lightly - no way! When I travel, I take everything I want, not just what I need. But in this case, nobody said a word. I think my mother-in-law had an idea that we were on our way, and the truth of our plans did eventually come out.

There was an awkward silence for a few days. Then Gerry said, "We'll both tell her, come on, I'll open a bottle of wine, then break the news to her *again*."

The news was out and there were tears, but gradually Gerry's mother accepted the situation. "You will be able to visit us." I said feebly.

PART 3

A New Life in Spain

The Journey South

So we were off! We packed up all we could fit into an estate car leaving the rest behind and left for Spain. Our car was fairly new, and totally loaded down with clothes for every occasion, with the exception of wellies! We had a few pots and pans and our warm Welsh wool blankets, which seemed like madness when I think about it, but they did come in handy when we lived briefly in Madrid.

Friends and neighbours thought we were a little crazy... perhaps we were. The family were all crying their eyes out - it was such a long way away. To us it all just seemed like a big adventure. After many tears, kisses and hugs, we left the following day. We didn't have any special plans. It was just a case of 'head south.'

We wanted to take our time on the journey; there was nothing to stop us. We both loved travelling; to pull in for a coffee or a jug of wine, a pit stop somewhere along the way was always on the agenda. After we crossed the Channel, we drove through the Basque Country, enjoying some memorable meals on route, down to Burgos, Valladolid, then avoiding the capital of Madrid, down past Cordoba to the southern coast of Spain and the Costa del Sol.

We drove right through Spain to Andalusia. Gerry was never keen on flying, so we travelled everywhere by car. We had a contact through the Masonic Society with someone who offered to rent us what we thought was an apartment in Fuengirola. The coast was a very different place in those days. Not only was there no motorway, there were hardly any cars. Most people travelled about by donkey.

Our new accommodation turned out to be a small white-washed cottage looking straight out onto the sparkling sea of Los Boliches. It was a true fisherman's village, and our neighbour even kept a cow. We were stunned when we realized the beast was kept in the house at night! Looking back, it was all very primitive, we had running water, and that was practically it.

Los Boliches was a tiny village. There were only about five thousand people living in the whole of Fuengirola. There was just one shop that sold everything out of barrels and crates. It was all just raw, local produce. We were right on the beach, and we took advantage of it. In those days everyone used deck chairs on the beach, no loungers or sun-beds. You had to take your own chairs and umbrellas. In those days the only foreigners we met seemed to be English aristocrats. It was always "Lord and Lady so and so..." We met some of them on our very first day on the Coast in a bar named Jacks in a small square in Fuengirola...

Above and opposite page: Images along the sands of Fuengirola and Los Boliches in 1965.

Above and below: Fuengirola as it was when we arrived in the 60s.

Hello 60s Spain

I remember clearly the day that Gerry and I arrived in what was then the small village of Fuengirola. There wasn't a soul around, even in the centre of town. Gerry parked the car and we walked slowly through the narrow streets until we came to a small square. "It's very quiet." I said in a whisper. A few curtains twitched very gently, but there were so few signs of life. We later realised we had forgotten about *siesta* time...

Suddenly we heard a few voices. "Follow that sound," said Gerry. From the corner of the square we heard people chatting from inside the one and only bar that was open. "They sound English." I said. We hesitated in the doorway when a man rose to his feet and, in a booming deep and cultured voice said, "Do come in my dears." Lord Rowallen introduced himself to us. I'll never forget the tone of his distinctive and welcoming words.

It didn't take us long to get to know the small group of Brits who had come to live in this area of Spain. Most of them had moved here from the colonies and were mainly architects, engineers, sons and heirs, or strangely enough, Old Etonians; well travelled, professional people who had lived in countries such as the Congo, China and India. All had a story to tell, a fascinating mix of people. Strangely there were few women, mainly men who were rather eccentric and generally very amusing. They seemed to know each other from their school days. Most were middle aged or retired, they wore Panama hats, and sat in deck chairs, sipping red wine and eating olives.

After only a few hours the ice was broken; from that moment the local expats took to us. They liked to see young people. It was not really a club, just Jack's bar, where they all gathered. Every afternoon we would wander down to meet people and have a little session. We virtually lived there; it was the only place to go. I also remember meeting one or two members of the Guinness family during those first few months.

We discovered a few other watering holes; One day a fellow who was an excellent horseman, decided to ride along the long empty beach. It was rather unusual, but nobody said a word, he eventually returned beaming from ear to ear, got off his grey mare and led her to a bar called 'No.10' where it was commonplace for riders to tie their horses up outside. Both man and beast enjoyed their refreshments!

When I look back on it all, I feel highly privileged to have known these lovely people. Jack was schooled at Eton. There was no snobbery and they were wonderful hosts, but they let it be known that you had to be accepted into the group. The men folk were gentlemen to the core. Remembering those days makes me feel good.

NB. If I had really known who she was at the time, I would have stopped to talk to the very attractive blonde lady whom I saw on Fulham High Street. There was something about her, something familiar that made me turn around to have a second look. I wasn't the only one. It's quite strange how people and names come back to you, not necessarily at the time; it might be the next day, or even a few months later. There was something familiar about her... Was she maybe a friend of my sister? I knew there was a likeness. I thought, it will come back to me and then I picked up a newspaper and there she was again. This attractive lady turned out to have been born plain George Jamieson, the first Briton to have a sex change. Coincidentally she became the wife of Lord Rowallen's son, the Hon. Arthur Corbett, later, 3rd Baron Rowallan.

Gerry Does What He Knows Best

When we first arrived in Spain, we didn't work for a time. We had sold the business, and were comfortably off. After a while, Gerry went back to what he knew best, working in advertising and distribution of newspapers, and he was offered a job back with the *Mail*. That was in 1966, and we lived in Madrid for a while. Gerry was involved in the distribution of papers such as the *Daily Mail* and *Financial Times* and I was accredited by the International Press Club to write freelance for the *Daily Mail* and other publications. I wrote a series of articles for the BBC and did the occasional TV broadcast for BBC Wales.

We used to drive around Spain introducing people to the *Daily Mail*; Gerry would drive up dusty unmade roads, through deserted countryside, to remote smallholdings just to deliver the latest newspaper. There was always someone in these *pueblos* who was English and gradually people came to rely on the paper. Bit by bit, he built up the readership. It was the first English newspaper in Andalusia. There were hardly any cars in the area and whenever we went up into the hills to deliver papers, people would come out of their houses and wave.

Life in the cottage by the beach was primitive. The milk arrived in the churn; it was goat's milk. There was a local shop, but it was small and had a limited range of goods. It was not even easy to recognize that it was a shop as it looked just like a normal house but with a bead curtain across the open doorway. Inside it was like a bazaar. All the foodstuffs were sold loose, stored in barrels; everything came in bulk and was measured out for you. There was no tea and only local wine, which we soon got used to. We lived mostly on *chorizo* and fish we bought directly from the fishermen, often mackerel. We would go down on to the beach and wait for them to come in with their catch; there were lots of fishing boats in those days.

People liked to go to Gibraltar to buy groceries. However, the Spanish Border had been closed on General Franco's orders in 1969, in response to the Gibraltar Constitution Order when the Gibraltarians voted overwhelmingly in favour of remaining British.

Gerry and I had learned some Spanish before we left England and we went to evening classes to get the basics so we could talk to everyone. Welsh people are very friendly and the locals soon spoke to us in a mixture of Spanish and English. Our Spanish neighbours would pop round for a chat and they never came empty-handed; always bringing a gift of some oranges or olives. One neighbour had a donkey and several chickens. At night they would take the donkey indoors; donkeys were the main means of travel and used for transporting goods to and from the market. They had to be well looked after!

One Christmas we were returning to England to stay with some friends, so we went next door to say goodbye and try to explain in our poor Spanish that we were going abroad. Our neighbour said, "My niece lives over the seas. She sings. Her name is Victoria de Los Angeles. Have you heard of her?" Of course we had heard of her - at the time she was one of *the* greatest opera singers in the world!

An Encounter with El Generalísimo

It was some time in the 60s and Spain's ruler, General Francisco Franco and his wife were coming to the Costa del Sol on an official visit. Everyone knew that they were coming. The press were all hoping for a scoop. Some people wanted to see them, some didn't. "Why not" I thought? He was a General, a man of power, a man who evoked fear, the man who had taken charge of Spain by force. News of his visit to the Costa del Sol awoke great anticipation.

We heard that, aside from viewing the progress of the hotels and apartments mushrooming along the coast, he would be playing a game of golf in Malaga. So early in the morning, we headed to one of the best golf courses in the south of Spain, to try and catch a glimpse of this infamous figure and his wife Doña Carmen. There were few people around; it was, no doubt, a private visit. There were dozens of plain clothed police and a few *guardias* around even in this select area.

We drove to the far end of the golf course, and to my astonishment, I saw Franco emerging from the group. At this moment I felt a bit lost, but shortly afterwards, his wife appeared. She was elegant and charming. Was I dreaming all of this or was it real? Franco was not in uniform but was looking rather dapper in his golf attire. I didn't dare speak; I felt more than a little overwhelmed.

His wife was quite beautiful, with lovely features. They made a handsome pair. We exchanged glances and then realising I was an *extranjera,* he smiled courteously and nodded in my direction. I exchanged a few words with his wife about the *Daily Mail* and then they vanished as briskly as they had arrived, whisked along the palm-fringed fairway with their entourage.

Above: The Gongora Bodega which Gerry represented, purveying wines around Southern Spain with great *gusto* in the 1960s.

Selling Wine for the Spaniards

During our trips around the Spanish countryside Gerry and I always liked to try the local wines. He was becoming quite a connoisseur.

On one of our outings, Gerry came across a company called Jose Gallego Gongora SA, at Villanueva del Riscal near Seville, a traditional wine producing *bodega*. We were invited in for a tour and tasting session. We got on very well with the hosts and realising Gerry was a natural salesman, they offered him a job as a representative of the *bodega*. He jumped at the chance and we travelled far and wide to promote Gongora's wines. We came to know the family intimately and become good friends.

Gongora is a true family business, handed down from generation to generation. The *bodegas* were founded in the year 1682 by Rafael de Gongora y Delgado and their family. Today, they are still in the old Hacienda de Para de Hierro, in Villa del Ariscal Sevilla, Spain. They are best known for their oak barrel aged fine wines known as *fino,* and their *amontillados*, creams and other liqueurs. Located in Aljarafe, the village takes its name from the Arabic word meaning, viewing point. However, the name Gongora didn't catch on too quickly and created some amusement with the expats, but the wine went down very well. After every visit to Seville we left with a car full of Gongora wines and plenty of tall orders!

New Adventures

When we first arrived on the Costa del Sol in the 60s, it was still Franco's Spain. Tourism was just taking a hold, and it was a good time to seize opportunities. We enjoyed our work on the papers, but still had some money from the sale of the business to invest...

Roasting on the Beach!

We eventually tired of living the good life in our humble fisherman's cottage, and in a moment of madness decided to move down the coast and open a restaurant serving typically British Sunday roast lunches. The restaurant, called Las Banderas, was located in the Marbesa area. Funnily enough, another famous Banderas can be found there these days, the Hollywood superstar, Malaga-born Antonio Banderas and his equally famous wife, Melanie Griffith have a luxurious beachfront villa in this very neighbourhood.

It was quite something running a restaurant back in the 70s in Spain. We ran it for three or four years, and it was very successful. Sundays were the big day when we cooked full roast lunches right there on the beach!

Gerry would do the big shop in the mornings at the Fuengirola market getting the best meat and vegetables for the Sunday lunches. We would buy carrots by the sack load and purchase the freshest fish directly from the boats in Fuengirola port. The roasts would be followed by homemade apple crumble and custard. The cooking was incredibly hard work, and there weren't even any English supermarkets in those days.

Our restaurant Las Banderas was a huge hit from day one. The British expats flocked there to enjoy the sumptuous roasts which I cooked myself for more than 50 covers in each sitting. Clients would turn up in their Jaguars and Roll-Royces to the beach. One day we had half a dozen Rollers parked outside. It was quite a picture!

Gerry, of course, was front-of-house, and he *loved* that! I would be stuck in the kitchen all day, while Gerry was schmoozing the guests, chatting and knocking back the wine; he was a natural host. I cringe at the thought of it. I could have killed him half the time!

We also ran a bar in the Hotel Artola near Cabopino and a pub in Pueblo Andaluz Fuengirola. Gerry particularly enjoyed being in the hospitality business. We met hundreds of people, made many friends and created momentum for our next venture, starting up our own English newspaper...

The Good Life with Gerry

Gerry was far too good-looking, he liked the ladies and the ladies liked him... It caused me quite a bit of grief over the years, but we were happily married for over 40 years...

Gerry had the gift of the gab, he was a natural-born salesman, you couldn't shut him up! It was definitely one of his virtues. Wherever he went, he caused a stir and created a following. This was all good news for starting up *SUR in English*!

While we ran our restaurant in Marbesa, Gerry was well suited to being front-of-house. It was very successful, more by accident than design... Gerry was never the stay-at-home type. He was very sociable and loved to be out and about.

We also entertained regularly at home in our villa in Calahonda. It was called *Nyth Eryr*, Welsh for eagle's nest. We had many a happy time with friends and family hosting dinner parties and barbecues practically all year round. Sometimes Gerry would cook, but more often than not, it was me cooking up a storm with my tried and tested recipes from my food column in the *SUR in English*...

And Gerry loved his nights out... possibly a bit too much! He certainly worked hard and played hard. For many years we would go to most of the *ferias* along the Coast; but always Fuengirola, Marbella and Mijas. Usually we dressed in the appropriate *feria* attire. It was great fun, especially if you went along with your own little crowd. Gerry enjoyed the atmosphere; the horses, wine, women and song - not necessarily always in that order!

We enjoyed life together in Spain, and would do the rounds of the restaurants popular with the expats; Club Oceano, Valparaiso, Albert's, Harbour Lights, Mijas Playa, Hamilton's, Toni Dalli's etc. Certainly we made the most of what was on offer and met some famous faces along the way, Billy Cotton, Sir Harry Secombe, Sir Cliff Richard, Sean Connery, Acker Bilk, Dennis Taylor, Keith Floyd. We were never into golf, but would cover the events and galas and have a good time!

PART 4

The *SUR in English* Years

A Good Idea Waiting to Happen

With Gerry's background in media, he had been a 'newspaperman' since leaving Llandovery College, and with my experience on the *Daily Mail*, we always had a hunch we would launch a paper in Spain.

With such a large population of English-speaking foreign residents on the Costa del Sol, all wanting to know what is happening in their neck of the woods, there was a ready made market of people crying out for a local paper to keep them abreast of local and international news.

Putting together a newspaper is not as easy as it sounds. Where will the finance come from? Several entrepreneurs had the same idea of starting a publication, but one by one, they fell apart and lost money. We made a mock up of what we thought people wanted, something to suit everyone. A newspaper is part and parcel of people's lives. It is an instrument of information; where to go, what's on, what to buy and where to eat.

Weighing up the pros and cons, we looked at every conceivable angle to consider the logistics of the business, funding being the main issue. We made a decision to go to publishers, Prensa Malagueña in Malaga. Surprisingly, we were given an interview straight away with its then editors, Joaquín Marín and Juan Soto.

There was an immediate interest in our idea to start a new free English newspaper for the many British and English speaking expatriates, but no actual 'go-ahead' plans. After the third meeting, they said, "Come back in two weeks." "No, we'll be back in one!" said Gerry as he turned to leave.

On 20th July 1984, after a fairly problem free time putting the debut issue together, it was 'mission accomplished'. We were up all night to see the print run - a thrilling moment! And in the early hours, at long last the dream had become a reality. The newspaper was finally in print... *SUR in English* was born!

Hot off the press, we loaded the car to the brim and took as many copies as we could to all our friends and supporters who had encouraged or helped along the way. We delivered up and down the Coast, to towns, resorts and remote villages and hamlets, sometimes just leaving one copy in the village bar or shop. Wherever there were pockets of Brits, we introduced *SUR in English* to them. We were always on the road looking for stories, and advertisers. Advertising came rapidly. We had no doubt that our 'new baby' would grow and thrive.

20 th. to 26 th. July 1984
English edition NO. 1
MA-6-1958
Circulation OJD controlled.
Free copy

SUR in English

Director: Joaquin Marin

Edited by Prensa Malagueña
Avda. Doctor Marañón, 48
29009-Málaga
Tel. 393900
Télex 79013MLGA

The £1,6 million train crash

Watched by 1.000 people including M. Ps, a passenger train crashed into a nuclear fuel flask at 100 miles per hour, at Old Dalby, Leics. The idea of this was to prove that nuclear waste can be transported safely around Britain. The train which had no driver, was wrecked in the attempt to crack open the 48 ton flask which only suffered an inch wide gouge in its lid. The demonstration cost British Rail £1.6 million, but it was meant to reassure the public that the movement of radio active material was safe.

Miners' Union funds diverted

According to the Daily Express miner' leaders have paid tens of thousands of pounds of union funds into their own private banking accounts. The National Union of Mineworkers in South Wales have admitted paying their staff, as well as themselves, six months salary in advance. In sharp contrast, the miners are suffering very hard finacially.

B. B. C. Makes a profit

B. B. C. Enterprises made 20 million pounds on their sales abroad. This is for such programmes as the B. C. television series on Shakespeare, Fawlty Towers, Doctor Who, To the Manor Born, Great Little Railways and Bergerac. The best seller is «The Six Wives of Henry VIII»

Falklands: Argentina break off discussions

The Argentinian goverment today broke off the discussions held in Berne with Britain, regarding the Falklands. The Argentinian Ambassador Dante Caputo, representing the government of Raul Alfonsin stated on arrival at Buenos Aires that he took the action because London was not prepared sto recognise as part of the discussions, the restoration of the sovereighty of Argentine over the Australasian Islands.

In the early hours of yesterday afternoon, the British Foreingn Minister denied that the official discussions with Argentina had been broken off regarding the future of the Falklands.

To regress

The certainty is that until Buenos Aires gives notification, and London denies it, the Swiss government does not wish to make any statement. A Foreign Office spokesman said that «Our latest irfcrmatic» is that the discussions continue. They have not been terminated».

Margaret Thatcher

The situation is complicated because the Argentinian government have ordered the immediate return of their representatives to

Buenos Aires. On arrival at the airport, Dante Caputo read the official communique in front of more than 100 journalists.

The Discussions

The discussions between the two countries began in Berne on Wednesday night under «top secret conditions». The meeting between the British and Argentinian goverment.

As soon as the discussions started, the Argentinian delegation reiterated «the sovereing rights of their country over the disputed islands. The possible reccommencement of the discussions is seen as very difficult, in view of the fact that the «sovereignty» is the all important point from both sides, and constitutes the «basis of the controversy».

One of the fundamental points of the negotiations was the sequence of the Falklands war, and the conditions under which both countries could renew political and economical relations.

Maggie is slipping according to the polls

London

According to the results taken today of a poll taken by the Daily Telegraph, the Labour Party have increased their lead over the Conservative party from 0.05% to 1%.

There is still a long way to go if the opposition want to occupy No. 10 Downing St. in the 1988 elections. According to the Daily Telegraph the Conservatives have been losing votes rapidly.

In April this year 41% who responded to the Gallup Poll were in favour of Mrs. Thatcher's party. Whereas it has now dropped to 37.50%. However it is not the Labour party who have gained, but the Liberal and Social Democratic Alliance.

Mass murder in San Diego

SAN DIEGO (USA)
The biggest murder ever committed in the United States by a single person, occurred last Wednesday when a total of twenty people were killed.
James Oliver Huberty, 41 years of age and separated from his wife, fired indiscriminately at clients in a hamburger bar owned by McDonalds, and at anyone

that was in the vicinity. The massacre which has enraged the public occurred in San Diego, Southern California.

About 4.0 in the afternoon, Huberty, an unemployed security guard burst into «McDonalds and started firing with an automatic rifle and other arms for about ten minutes without

stopping. Meanwhile the terrorised clients tried to escape by any possible exit. There were seventeen victims within the building, including several children accompanied by their parents.

Immediately the killer left the building and killed two adolescents who were cycling past. The police

were alerted and Huberty once again took refuge in the hamburger bar. An armed policeman with a telescopic rifle shot him and put an end to the massacre. This latest mass killing has surpassed that committed by Charles Whitmen in 1966, who also with a rifle killed 16 people in the grounds of Texas University.

The province of Málaga.— Today we begin in this issue of SUR in english a series of reports dedicated to the province of Málaga. In these the reader will find the most important and interesting details of the localities and typical corners of the area. In this photograph by Salas we can appreciate the beatiful façade of Málaga Cathedral, a national monument constructed between the XV and XVI century. It's architectural makeup is the work of Díaz Palacios y Ortiz de Vargas and the sculptures by Pedro de Mena, who sculptured 40 out of the 58 arts of work, together with José de Micael. Visiting hours 10 to 13 and 16 to 17.20

It's a SUR-per day today

Today 20th July 1984 hails the birth of SUR in english. This is the first weekly give-away english language newspaper produced for the Costa del Sol.

We aim to provide in SUR in english as much information as possible and an advance programme of events on the Costa del Sol for our readers, which we hope to have with the cooperation of Don Joaquín Marin, Editor of SUR and his staff, local Town Halls and Tourist Boards, Hotels, Educational establishments, Entertainment and Sports centres, etc., and you the Public.

Please send us your ideas, your views and your comments. We want you to know what is going on so that you can enjoy all the facilities (not only the sun) that are available to you on the Costa del Sol. We thank you Kevin Keegan for your good whishes for a great Kick Off.

In this edition

Kevin Keegan plays golf in Mijas
Page 14

Spanish fiesta
Page 3

Horse Racing
Page 13

GIB. TV. programmes
Page 2

The Once a Week Colleagues

By Pedro Luis Gomez, Director of Publications, *Diario SUR*

I worked with Joan and Gerry Davies on *SUR in English* from day one. They were much loved. I was very young at the time; they were like parents to me.

One day they appeared in our offices with Jeff Kelly. They were such nice people, from the first day, and they fitted seamlessly into life here on the paper. They would turn up once a week with their portable typewriter and we would say, "What have you got for us today Gerry?" Then we'd get down to putting the paper together. Joan was the quieter of the two but she kept Gerry under control, as he liked to go out when he got the chance! He would nip out for a glass of wine, and she would get really cross!

They had to get by on what little Spanish they knew, as none of the staff spoke any English at all. They struggled to be understood at times, and would wonder if they were getting through to us correctly. I didn't have a clue about English - which led to some amusement. One day they had a news item entitled "Mass Murder in San Diego". I thought it meant, "*More* dead people in San Diego", and I said, "Will there be more dead people in Chicago too?!" Joan was almost hysterical and broke out in a fit of the hiccups then Gerry was slapping her on the back. It was hilarious, like a comedy sketch!

As *SUR in English* grew, and we had a few English speakers in the office, they became known as *El Peñon*, or The Rock, like Gibraltar. There was a student doing work experience, Clotti Berlanger. She spoke some English, and she would help Joan and Gerry out, making calls for them, buying things, and she would help Gerry find a parking space when he came to the office. He didn't really like driving and would get flustered by the Malaga traffic and get a bit lost in the one-way system. Clotti would go and stand on the corner of the street ready to guide them into a parking space.

Both Joan and Gerry had strong characters, and would have their run-ins. They were affectionately known as '*Los Roper*' in other words, 'George and Mildred' from the popular TV series of the same name. Some people still think of them that way. They typified the life of the foreign residents. When Gerry got wound up, his cheeks would go red and we used to say, "Joan, leave Gerry alone, he looks like *Gusi-Luz,*" the name of a doll with little red cheeks that you could buy at the time in Spain.

We had a great time working together. Joan and Gerry were the heart and soul of the *SUR in English*. We put down the tracks, and they drove the train. There was a strong bond between all the team; they were like parents to Liz, and the *SUR in English* quickly took off. Before we knew it, I was buying cakes to celebrate the 5th anniversary which we ate right here in the office.

The couple were an integral part of *SUR*, and it's funny, as they only came to the office one day a week, but they quickly found their way into our hearts. It's not like we lived in each other's pockets or travelled with them, but they were much loved.

SUR in English became a big success; financially, socially, professionally speaking. Joan and Gerry opened up a new world to us. They would introduce us to all kinds of characters, give us a window on the world of the foreign residents, people who had previously been out of reach living in their own urbanizations, with their own shops, restaurants and bars.

Joan was funny. I remember her recipes; she often used to get the quantities wrong. There would be too much flour, for example, but she loved baking cakes, and would often bring her goodies into the offices. They would arrive every Thursday, late afternoon, around 6pm, and would get on with putting the paper together. They would be there until about five or six in the morning. We would all go out to the bar for dinner Joan always ate *tortilla* and tomato and Gerry would have a sandwich, and sneak in a couple of shots of *anis*. I once bought him a bottle as a gift, and Joan was furious with me!

Gerry was larger than life; he had a big personality. Joan seemed to be overshadowed by him, but in actual fact, she kept him in check, especially when he lost his temper, which was quite frequent. One day we organized a trip for the readers. Joan and Gerry came along. Some of his family joined us; they were policemen. We were visiting the *Parador* in Malaga, and for some unknown reason, one of the readers turned terribly angry and started picking a fight with Gerry. So his relatives stepped in, arrested the guy and escorted him off to the police station.

Personally, I really love Joan and Gerry. They were a big part of my youth. When Gerry died, it was terribly sad. When I saw Joan at the cemetery she said, "I'm going to be really lonely without him." Nobody could have imagined that he would die so young. They had built up something so special with the paper, giving them financial stability, a wide social circle and status. They were invited to everything. People would hold events *just* to appear in *SUR in English*. It was a status they didn't really enjoy for long. Gerry died just 11 years after starting the paper. Afterwards, Joan continued to be a contributor, but it was never the same.

The day Gerry died, it was the first and only time we have had to say, "Stop the press!" and literally stop printing to re-run the paper with the news of his passing away. I remember the day Joan and Gerry appeared with Jeff Kelly, like it was yesterday, and now it's almost thirty years ago. They played a big part in my life.

We had a great time working together, they worked really hard going all over the coast, covering those events, developing the photos, delivering them to the office; there was nothing digital then, no mobiles, it was harder than it looked! As I said, Joan was quiet, partly because she was not fluent in Spanish. Like many foreign residents, even though they live here many years, they don't master the language. But it's just as well; if they all spoke Spanish, there would be no need for *SUR in English* anyway...

Above: Gerry and I in action with our trusty portable typewriter at the *SUR in English* offices in 1985.

Above: Gerry with a mock-up of the first front page.

The Friday Couple

In July 1989, coinciding with the 5th anniversary of *SUR in English*, *Lookout* magazine printed an article by Nigel Bowden about our success story:

When the annals of the Costa del Sol are written, Joan and Gerald Davies will be remembered as the couple who pioneered two commodities indispensable to expatriates living on the Coast; restaurants that serve traditional English Sunday lunches on the beach and freebie newspapers.

Joan and Gerry, as they are known, admit the credit for restaurant roasts may not be entirely theirs, but the couple's contribution to Spain's plethora of foreign language publications is undeniable.

Starting a newspaper was something Joan and Gerry had always wanted to do. Says Gerry, "I always thought there was a gap in the market on the Costa del Sol for a give-away paper."

The management of SUR, the provincial newspaper for Malaga quickly saw the potential. "Mind you," laughs Gerry, "The rest of the staff thought we were a bit of a joke when we started."

The newspaper industry is nothing new to Joan and Gerald Davies. Apart from running a sub-post office in Wales and various restaurants on the Costa del Sol, they have been involved with the printed word all their lives.

On the Cocktail Party Circuit with Joan & Gerry

by Friend and Press Colleague, Jack Nusbaum

I first met Joan and Gerry Davies some 30 years ago when the two of them came up with a brilliant, very special and unique weekly English addition to Spain's respected, long running newspaper, *Diario SUR*. They had gathered, clipped, cut, pasted and put together a layout, banner name, *SUR in English*, presented it to the publisher which was immediately latched onto, set up for weekly publication, and has gone from strength to strength, never a break, steadily since 1984.

Joan was given a fine position in the operation covering all kinds of events and special occasions on the Costa del Sol. As Joan's name grew in popularity and she was meeting all levels of company directors and influential people, as well as building a loyal list of *SUR in English* readers. Joan came up with still another terrific, hugely enjoyable and accepted weekly column of good home cooked recipes. This new column was given plenty of publishing space each week, half pages or more depending on what gourmet specials Joan wrote up.

Gerry had the responsibility of distributing the weekly *SUR in English* edition along the coast. Realizing the importance of assured placement, Gerry developed a fine dedication to this assignment and never, ever failed. In addition to his distribution and sales position, Gerry had to change hats and become Joan's chauffeur (presumably unpaid by Joan!) and take her all over the coast to carry out her editorial assignments.

Going back to when all kinds of real estate, golf clubs and commercial complexes began to mushroom over the entire coast, there were constant invitations for the media to launches and events.

I was publication director for *Costa Golf Magazine* and began to meet up with Joan and Gerry regularly at such events. Often Spanish presented a bit of a problem for them, but I knew a little Spanish so Joan hooked on to me for help: "Jack, who is that?" or "What was he saying?" "Do you know them?" "Can you introduce me?" An exchange of information would frequently take place.

Meantime, Gerry, with some experience of working for wine companies, among other jobs, became something of a wine connoisseur. Rather than just stand around looking good and doing nothing, he would always somehow manage to pick up a glass of red wine - his preference - take a sip or two, call me over to explain the vintage, the age, the region, etc., sipping as he spoke and finally, offer his opinion.

Opposite; With his familiar smile, Gerry the wine connoisseur, ready to top up the glasses at a house party in the 1980s.

Gerry had to time to kill while Joan gathered her stories and these wine-tasting sessions were most enjoyable. There would invariably be various *tapas* passed around by roving waiters and Gerry, naturally, loved nibbling as he sipped.

Our meetings at the regular press events forged a lifelong friendship as we enjoyed each other's company while writing up a storm. We would be handed press kits full of all kinds of promotional info that Joan would peruse and question me about, her ballpoint pen and notepads flying at high speed. Duly her write-ups would appear in the following edition of *SUR in English*. Often Gerry would deliver extra copies to the company involved, and heaps of praise would be piled on Joan for the splendid job she had done.

Above: Article about *SUR in English* at the Money Show published in *Diario SUR* in 1988. Gerry and I were photographed with the Mayor of Marbella, Alfonso Cañas.

Below: More recently, one of my many recipe features from *SUR in English*.

Asturian cooking on the Costa

ENRIQUE BELLVER

The lush and fresh scenery in Asturias is reflected in its gastronomy and in Arroyo de la Miel there is a restaurant which serves typical and authentic Asturian food.

Perhaps the most well known dish from the region, fabada (a stew made with white beans and chorizo), is as popular during the summer months as it is when the cold weather hits.

Other specialities well worth trying in Rincón Asturiana (Asturian corner) are the goat's cheese croquettes and 'Conchi's homemade cheesecake'.

RINCÓN ASTURIANO

▶ **Address:** Plaza de la Iglesia, 3, Arroyo de la Miel.
▶ **Telephone:** 952567628.
▶ **Open:** Everyday.
▶ **Average price:** 30 euros.

RECIPES TO CUT OUT AND KEEP

JOAN DAVIES

Cooking "en papillote"

HAM EN PAPILLOTE

▶ Half cup butter
▶ 6 slices cooked ham (1 cm. thick)
▶ Port
▶ Half cup sour cream
▶ Grated Parmesan

Melt the butter in a heavy-based pan and sauté the ham until they are lightly browned on both sides. Pour a little Port into the pan and let it thicken slightly. Transfer the ham to individual squares of foil. Stir the sour cream into the juices and pour over the ham. Sprinkle each steak with a little Parmesan cheese and wrap the foil tightly around it. Cook the steaks in a hot oven for 10-12 minutes and serve in the packets.

SALMON EN PAPILLOTE

▶ 4 small to medium cutlets of fresh salmon (1 per person)
▶ 8 thin slices of smoked ham (Serrano)
▶ butter
▶ lemon slices

For each serving butter a square of foil and place a slice of ham in the centre. Put a salmon cutlet on top then another slice of ham. Put a small chunk of butter and a slice of lemon on top of the sandwich and wrap the foil around it. Cook the packets in a hot oven for about 10-12 minutes or until fish is just cooked through. Serve in the foil with steamed new potatoes and a garnish of chopped parsley.

APRICOT WHIP

▶ 250g. dried apricots
▶ 2 heaped tbsps. sugar
▶ half cup sweet sherry
▶ 2 egg whites, beaten
▶ 2 heaped tbsps. sugar
▶ half cup heavy cream
▶ slivers of toasted almond

Soak the apricots in a pan of cold water for several hours. Stir in the sugar and cook over low heat until tender. Drain the apricots and cook the syrup until it forms a thick glaze. Stir the glaze back into the apricots and leave to cool. Pour in the sherry and puree the mixture until smooth. Beat the egg whites until stiff, and slowly fold into the mixture together with the cream. Spoon into tall dessert glasses and chill thoroughly. Before serving sprinkle the top with the slivers of toasted almonds.

TUNA COCKTAIL

▶ 1 can tuna (200)
▶ 150g natural yoghurt
▶ 2 tbsps. tomato ketchup
▶ 2 tbsps. lemon juice
▶ 1 tbsp. Worcester sauce
▶ 3 heaped tbsps. grated cucumber
▶ 1 lettuce heart, chopped
▶ Tabasco (optional)

Divide the chopped lettuce and into four large wine glasses. Mix together the ketchup, yoghurt, lemon juice, Worcester sauce and cucumber in a bowl. Add a few dashes of Tabasco (optional). Drain the tuna, and divide into small chunks and add to the mixture. Finally, mix it well and then spoon into the glasses. Serve chilled.

Above: Gerry looks on as I cut into the 5th Anniversary cake with Liz Parry, Pedro Luis Gomez, Eve Browne and the *SUR in English* team.

JOAN & GERRY Davies

The Heart and Soul of *SUR in English*

by Louise Cook Edwards

If a week in politics is like a year, that first few months on *SUR in English* must have felt like a lifetime to Joan and Gerry who were really the Heart and Soul of the paper. The very first edition of *SUR in English* on 20th July 1984 featured the conflict with UK and Argentina; a news item entitled 'Argentina Breaking off Discussions' which Joan had written. A journalist should never feel obliged to reveal his or her sources, but in those days, Joan must have been relying on the daily British press or the BBC World Service as she had little or no access to news wires, or other official channels.

The paper started out as it meant to go on, with a mix of international news stories and lifestyle pieces from Andalusia. Also in the first edition, Joan wrote a travel piece entitled 'A Romantic Train Ride' about the journey between Algeciras and Ronda; on the railway lines built by British aristocrats and engineers. Also in the first weekly edition, which was a skinny 16 pages, was a full-page advertisement for San Miguel beer, (overleaf) very fitting as one of Gerry's first big clients, fond as he was of a few glasses of the now iconic Spanish beer.

SUR in English certainly delivered an eclectic array of local, Spanish and international news; stories to appeal to expat tastes. Political news shared pages with photographs of scantily clad actresses, and the timetable of bullfights at Malaga's bullring, along with advertising for Spanish lessons taught in the intensive, progressive method, whatever that might be...

A Social Whirl

These were exciting times for Joan and Gerry, who quickly began to document the Costa's vibrant expat social scene, complete with the jet-set parties and galas of the rich and famous international set - parties at which Joan would rub shoulders with a suave Sean Connery, or glamorous Britt Ekland, along with the European *crème de la crème* including Marbella residents, Countess Gunilla von Bismarck, Philippe Junot, Manolo Santana and Adnan Khashoggi all of whom spent at least part of the year in the luxurious resort of Marbella.

In issue 5 of *SUR in English*, when the holiday season was in full swing, Joan reported on a Stevie Wonder concert coming up at the Marbella Football Stadium, tragedies of people dying in the UK miners strikes, and a private visit by the King of Spain to the England, hosted by Lord Strathmore, cousin of the Queen Mother.

In the last week of August 1984, Joan reported on Malaga being the number one gastronomic city in Andalusia and wrote about a scandal concerning Madrid police; holidaying members of the force were discovered moonlighting as bodyguards for the wealthy Arabs in Marbella. These early editions are gems that crystallized the mind-set of the foreign residents of the time. Life appeared to be a hedonistic blend of sport, leisure and socializing with golf tournaments, sailing classes, concerts and Rotary Club dinners, along with the occasional piece of non-news, such as a picture of Sophia Loren arriving at Heathrow airport with her son...

A Recipe for Success

With such diverse content, the new weekly paper was opening up a world of possibilities not just to Joan and Gerry, but also to the entire readership of English speaking Costa del Sol residents. By September, just three months after launching *SUR in English*, Joan started incorporating her own recipe page, featuring such headlines as 'A Peach of a Dish', or a classic recipe for that quintessentially British tipple, Pimms.

The paper kept the foreign residents informed of what was going on in Spain; surrealist icon Salvador Dali was to undergo an operation, and Paquirri, a good-looking young bullfighter, was gored to death, leaving his glamorous young widow, singer Isabel Pantoja, totally distraught. Years later, ghosts would come back to haunt her in Marbella, but not for the same reasons.

The weekly dose of *SUR in English* gave a tantalizing picture of what life was like for Joan and Gerry who had embarked upon a publishing adventure in a foreign land, not exactly in the first flush of youth, and were giving it everything they had. Joan started to report on the local cultural scene, the plays and functions at the Salon Varietes theatre in Fuengirola, the *ferias* in Mijas and Nerja. The close links with the parent Spanish newspaper, *Diario SUR* were evident in a story about Ian and Mignon Walters, an English couple that had taught themselves Spanish in a year by reading their daily copy of *Diario SUR*.

Joan and Gerry found themselves at the very heart of expat life, reporting on anything and everything; An English wedding at the grand church of *La Encarnación* in Marbella's quaint Old Town, allusions to the 'Costa del Crime' with a story about 'The Gent', a thief from Torremolinos who flew to London to commit a robbery and ended up getting jailed for 16 years. There was also an article about the false claim of an art theft of several Picassos from a luxury yacht moored in Puerto Banus.

Opposite: San Miguel advertisement in the first edition of *SUR in English.*

Servicing the Community

The paper became increasingly useful to the foreign community as businesses flocked to advertise, and provide good solid advice to the frequently uninitiated foreigners abroad, with articles on how to create a company, and a list of legally registered estate agents in the area. There was also a curious letter published from a tourist to the Mayor of Malaga. It complained how the British press always focused on the negative aspects of life in Spain, while singing the praises of the area and congratulating the Mayor on presiding over such a fabulous place.

Also within the first few months of *SUR in English*'s life, was a piece about a presentation in Madrid of a campaign by the Regional Tourist Board entitled, 'Andalusia, Golden Days'. The Tourist Board was promoting activities to entice tourists to come and enjoy the sunshine in the low season. 30 years on, some things just never change.

It was only a few months into the life of the newspaper, when the classified section was added to *SUR in English* - something that would become invaluable for the practicalities of life for the foreign community, and which would divide opinion on whether or not the paper really ought to include the rather explicit and controversial 'red light' section. Joan however, would often place little ads and comments in the classifieds, wishing everyone a Merry Christmas, for example!

Celebrity Status and Monkey Business

Joan clearly threw herself into life on the thriving Costa del Sol, finding increasingly fun assignments, such as interviewing Britt Ekland about her role in the 1985 movie, *Marbella - Un Golpe de Cinco Estrellas*. Featuring Britt, Rod Taylor and Fernando Fernán Gomez, it was partly filmed in an English-run Marbella antique shop, called Portobello. Around this time the Costa del Sol was a magnet for filmmakers, and since then literally hundreds of directors have used the coast as a movie backdrop.

In the 30th November 1984 edition, news that the border of Gibraltar and Spain would finally be opened up after fifteen years following the signing of the Brussels Agreement, shared the headlines with a story about some escaped chimpanzees from Fuengirola Zoo giving the local police the run around.

Above: Original film poster from the 1985 movie, *Marbella - Un Golpe de 5 Estrellas*, featuring Britt Ekland.
I briefly interviewed Britt during a break from filming.

Above: Captain Mark Phillips lays a foundation stone in Sotogrande in 1994.

Left: Sean Connery KBE with wife Micheline, taking home a golf trophy. c.1985.

Below: A fresh faced Stephen Hendry MBE with fellow snooker player Dennis Taylor at a Costa Gala dinner in 1989.

Top left: Belle, Eve Browne, me and Kate with
                 Christer Melkerson of Svenska Magazine.

Top right: Enjoying a BBQ lunch with the
                 charming celebrity chef Keith Floyd
                 in 1987.

Above: Head master of EIC, Ron Griffin
                 and photographer Patrick Lichfield
                 at a school event in 1998.

Above right: Englebert Hemperdink in the 1980s

Right: Me with Luigi of the popular bar of
                 the same name in Marbella.

Above: Acker Bilk after his show, Salon Varietes launch - 1985.

Top right: Wimbledon champ, Manolo Santana in his club at the Puente Romano Hotel with Philippe Junot. Note the open fields in the distance. c.1978.

Right: With Count Rudi von Schoenburg, the face of the Marbella Club Hotel and the former owner of the Don Carlos Hotel, Jihad El Khoury at the launch of the Richard Ellis Building. Marbella 1995.

Below: Alfonso von Hohenlohe with Actress Romy Schneider and three times F1 Champion Jackie Stewart OBE. c.1973.

Not six months had passed when *SUR in English* succumbed to demand and started placing advertising in lucrative slots on the front cover. Before the end of 1984, Joan would get to report on a thrilling event - the landing of Concorde in Malaga and also the Peter Allis Concorde Golf Tournament where Joan would get to mingle with many film stars and A-list celebrities. Robert Powell, Kevin Keegan, Jimmy Tarbuck and Bobby Charlton, were amongst the long list of celebs staying at the luxurious 5-star Los Monteros Hotel, raising money at the lavish charity gala. The winners were awarded Concorde shaped trophies.

Gerry's interests would also be reflected in the weekly paper, the rugby results of a Spain - Tunisia match, along with the British football results. Joan and Gerry had their fingers on the pulse of the expat scene and if *SUR in English* became virtually an overnight success, it was because the couple's tastes and interests typified those of the foreign community and they gave them exactly what they wanted.

In the 21st December edition that year, the paper printed King Juan Carlos's Christmas message. And in the recipe section for the Christmas edition, Joan wrote, "Christmas is the time for giving, for receiving and for sharing. It is a happy time, with lots of gaiety, fun and pleasure. It's party time!"

And it *was* party time, in more ways than one. Joan and Gerry worked hard and put in exceptionally long hours to bring everyone the best of expat life on the Coast, they were caught up in a social whirl, gaining huge respect and making the paper an huge success.

Good for Business

By the time *SUR in English* celebrated its 5th anniversary in 1989, Marbella had a new Mayor - the controversial Jesus Gil y Gil, and Joan was delivering a lot more social news and doing interviews with residents reflecting on their Costa lifestyles. From its humble beginnings with just 6,000 copies printed of the first issue, by then, *SUR in English* had a staggering 48,326 copies coming off the press as recorded by the OJD, the official body for newspaper distribution in Spain.

Flicking through the pages of previous editions of *SUR in English* is to relive the history of the expatriate community in the context of life in Spain. It is all in the mix. On 19th July 1989, Joan was reporting on the smoking restrictions that would soon be introduced to Andalusia; Julio Iglesias's ex-wife, Isabel Preysler and her politician husband, Miguel Boyer being pursued by paparazzi while holidaying in Marbella and the Marbella Town Hall organizing the annual Moraga; a free barbecued sardine fest to celebrate the *Día del Carmen*, the patron of fishermen.

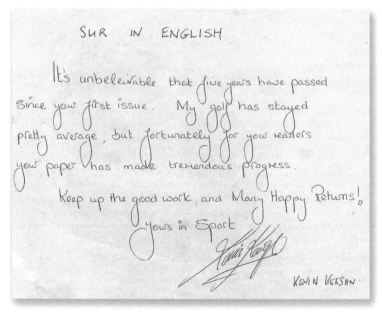

SUR IN ENGLISH

It's unbelievable that five years have passed since your first issue. My golf has stayed pretty average, but fortunately for your readers your paper has made tremendous progress.

Keep up the good work, and Many Happy Returns!

Yours in Sport

KEVIN KEEGAN

Above: Kevin Keegan OBE with his wife Jean and daughter Laura in 1981 and Letter from Kevin, sent to me at *SUR in English.*

Right: Me with my friend Joan Janes.

Below: Enjoying *canciones de La Tuna* during a private cocktail party at Marbella's Melia Don Pepe Hotel.

A double-page advertisement for Cortefiel clothing indicates that Spanish businesses were getting wise to the spending power of the foreign community, and placing their advertising budgets in publications that promised a good return. *SUR in English*'s clientele vied for those coveted spaces on the front page where thousands of pairs of eyes were trained weekly, all looking for tips on how to spend their time and their pounds, pesetas or kronor.

This same year, the paper reported news that British criminals would be extradited from Spain when caught by the Spanish authorities, and that Norwegians and Swedes would be allowed to vote in the Spanish elections. Again the foreign pound, dollar or deutschmark were paving the streets of the Costa del Sol with gold, and for Joan and Gerry, and the paper's Spanish owners, this was all exceptionally good news.

Gibraltar began to feature more heavily in the newspaper, along with weighty adverts for banks and financial institutions on The Rock, and so successful was *SUR in English*, that regular special subject advertising supplements would be placed in the paper to keep up with demand. These supplements gained considerable approval from the Spanish authorities that realized their role in promoting the glories of Andalusia and the Costa del Sol, particularly at trade fairs abroad.

In July 1989, the paper celebrated the success of its first five years, with a prize draw inviting readers to enter a survey, and win a trip around Andalusia; Jerez, Sevilla, Granada and Barrio de Santa Cruz in Cadiz. In that same edition was a full-page ad for a Julio Iglesias concert and a plea from the Spanish health authorities asking tourists to become blood donors. With a floating expat population reaching hundreds of thousands in the height of the summer, the blood of the locals would presumably no longer be copious enough to go round.

Through the 80s Joan and Gerry's role on *SUR in English* took them far and wide. Gerry was not keen on air travel, so his colleagues would represent the paper at events such as the World Travel Market in London and members of staff were invited on press trips to luxurious resorts such as Henlow Grange. In the society pages, Joan reported on the visits of illustrious guests such as Baroness Carmen Thyssen, who owns a mansion in Marbella, and was frequently seen at galas and the most select private parties.

Following pages: Feature published about the 10th anniversary edition. Portrait of Gerry and me on the Cunard Princess in 1994.

Happy birthday

SUR in English celebra hoy con una fiesta su décimo aniversario

MALAGA ■ Hoy se entonará un ruidoso «Happy birthday» en SUR. Es el cumpleaños de SUR in English, que celebra su X aniversario con la satisfacción de haber alcanzado grandes cotas y con la ilusión de que, por su juventud, aún se pueden lograr muchas más. Cuando a finales de 1983 surgió el proyecto de hacer un periódico en inglés, nadie podía imaginarse que la idea se convertiría en un gran éxito una década después. Hasta aquel entonces, en la Costa del Sol habían proliferado periódicos que nunca superaron unas audiencias mínimas y pronto desaparecieron e incluso en la mayoría de los diarios locales, en épocas diversas, se había puesto de moda editar una o dos páginas con noticias en inglés, que ni satisfacían a los ingleses ni a los lectores habituales. La experiencia, pues, no tenía precedentes, salvo en Palma de Mallorca. Lo que sí se sabía es que una amplísima colonia de habla inglesa estaba necesitada de un vehículo de comunicación y que si se acertaba en el producto, éste podía tener un futuro.

El futuro de aquel proyecto, que salió a la calle por primera vez en la tercera semana de julio de 1984, es hoy una gran realidad: SUR in English, edición en inglés —que no suplemento— de SUR que se distribuye todos los viernes, ha alcanzado los 48.000 ejemplares de tirada —regulado por OJD (Oficina de Justificación de la Difusión)—, con una audiencia media estimada de 230.000 personas. Su campo de influencia, que abarca toda Andalucía y Levante, Gibraltar, Melilla, Ceuta, Madrid y Barcelona, lo ha convertido en apenas dos lustros en el periódico en lengua inglesa de mayor difusión en la Europa continental.

«Desde que surgió la idea la acogimos con entusiasmo, pese a que sabíamos que las experiencias anteriores de publicaciones similares habían fracasado. Pero entendimos que merecía la pena probar, entre otras cosas porque vimos que era el momento óptimo tras un concienzudo estudio del proyecto», afirma Juan Soto, director general de Prensa Malagueña, quien recuerda con cariño aquellos momentos iniciales de SUR in English. «Tras madurar el proyecto, aprovechamos un viaje que hicimos el director, Joaquín Marín, y yo a Londres para estudiar in situ varias publicaciones gratuitas. Como se sabe, en el mercado anglosajón la

prensa gratuita juega un papel importante, pero aquí no había experiencia al respecto».

Aquella visita fue muy importante porque se centró en el proyecto desde el punto de vista administrativo y gerencial. Al ser gratuito, igualmente, se tuvo que estudiar un método alternativo de distribución, lo que se realizó también de forma detallada y ambiciosa.

Una vez puestos los mimbres organizativos había que estructurar el periódico en sí. «No había antecedentes directos, por lo que el resultado era imprevisible, señala Joaquín Marín, director de SUR y editor in chief de SUR in English, «pero nosotros apostamos fuerte desde el primer momento por este proyecto. Aportamos toda nuestra estructura, todo nuestro conocimiento y todo nuestro entusiasmo».

Pedro Luis Gómez, redactor jefe de SUR y deputy editor in chief de SUR in English, fue encargado como responsable de suplementos de la puesta en marcha del proyecto: «El principal problema era articular algo sobre lo que no teníamos ningún antecedente. ¿Cómo hacerlo? Había distintas posibilidades, pero nos decidimos desde el primer momento por la que entendíamos que podía tener éxito: hacer un periódico semanal para la colonia de habla inglesa que sirviera de nexo de unión entre ellos mismos y con la sociedad que la rodea», señala.

Para Joaquín Marín, una de las claves del éxito está en que se hizo un periódico para los ingleses pero con mentalidad española. Lo que pasa en Gran Bretaña o en otros países de su influencia no es noticia de portada para nosotros, salvo hechos muy concretos. La noticia que se publica en SUR in English afecta a esa colonia, bien porque ellos sean los protagonistas o porque les puede afectar de alguna manera».

Juan Soto recuerda que «pocos creían que el proyecto cuajaría, y sin embargo hoy todos elogian el producto que sale a la calle, que, además, se ha convertido en un vehículo publicitario de primera magnitud. Lo cierto es que hoy, que se cumple el X aniversario de SUR in English, para todos nosotros es un gran orgullo la trayectoria seguida en este tiempo y las cotas alcanzadas. Ahora nuestro objetivo es que, cada día más, SUR in English se convierta en el gran perió-

dico en lengua inglesa de España».

TRAYECTORIA

Aquel proyecto, que salió a la calle el 20 de julio de 1984, ha visto cómo ha crecido de forma impensable entonces. De aquellas 16 páginas se han pasado a las 64 de esta semana; de aquellos 10.000 ejemplares iniciales se ha pasado a los casi 50.000; de aquella difusión incierta se ha llegado a cotas casi impensables, cercanas a las 250.000 personas; de aquel pequeño periódico semanal se ha pasado a un periódico en toda la extensión de la palabra, con redacción propia, con sistemas de autoedición propios, con equipo de publicidad y administración propios...

Hoy en día, SUR in English cuenta con una plantilla perfilada, en la que Liz Parry, que entró a formar parte de esta publicación en 1985, y Eva Browne, que lo hizo en 1991, forman parte fundamental. Liz Parry, actual editor de la publicación, considera que «la fórmula de redacción en SUR in English puede parecer sencilla, pero en realidad no lo es. Hay que intentar, por todos los medios,

competir con los grandes periódicos británicos, que no olvidemos están en la costa a las 10 de la mañana de cada día, y con los medios de comunicación audiovisuales, así que la fórmula para captar la atención del lector ha de ser diferente».

Eva Browne, advertising manager de la publicación —responsable de publicidad—, considera que «pocas publicaciones hay tan efectivas en el campo publicitario como SUR in English. Por ello se explican nuestras diez páginas de pequeños anuncios semanales o las campañas que nos remiten grandes compañías internacionales».

Gerry y Joan Davies, artífices de SUR in English en sus comienzos, recuerdan con afecto aquellos momentos: «Para nosotros ha sido una gran experiencia. Fueron momentos hermosos, aunque no exentos de dificultades». Gerry y Joan Davies mantienen su colaboración y su vínculo con SUR in English en la actualidad. La redacción se completa con Kate Rayner, mientras que Julia Oberg realiza actualmente prácticas y Jo Quintero es colaboradora. Ana María Reina desarrolla funciones de diseño publicitario y a la vez ejecuta temas administrativos, conjuntamente con Sonia González.

«Los objetivos están claros: servir a nuestros lectores con la rigurosidad, objetividad y eficacia como lo hemos hecho hasta ahora. Nuestra publicación es seguida con interés desde muchos sectores de la prensa española, y eso nos llena de orgullo», señala Joaquín Marín.

«El futuro es halagüeño, pero no podemos dormirnos en los laureles», especifica Juan Soto. «Tenemos que cumplir muchos objetivos propuestos que esperamos sean una grata realidad dentro de 10 años, cuando celebremos nuestro XX aniversario».

Todos los viernes, cientos de miles de personas esperan que llegue a sus manos SUR in English. Mediante un complejo pero a la vez efectivo sistema de distribución, el periódico llega fiel a su cita. Esta noche, en Benalmádena, se celebrará el X aniversario de la publicación con una fiesta a la que asistirán importantes personalidades de la Costa del Sol y del mundo de la comunicación tanto de España como de otros países. Será el momento de entonar el «Happy birthday».

ANTONIO SALAS
Sentados, Juan Soto (izquierda) y Joaquín Marín; de pie, de izquierda a derecha, Sonia González, Julia Oberg, Ana María Reina, Pedro Luis Gómez, Liz Parry, Eve Browne y Kate Rayner

Un periódico internacional

SUR in English es un periódico internacional. No sólo por sus lectores, de las más diversas nacionalidades, o porque se utilice como libro de texto en institutos y colegios así como en numerosas academias y universidades andaluzas donde se imparten clases de inglés, sino por su presencia en importantes eventos en distintos países de Europa, como Gran Bretaña, Alemania y Francia.

SUR in English ha realizado monográficos sobre la Costa del Sol, Málaga y Andalucía en las prestigiosas ferias de turismo Wolrd Travel Market de Londres, ITB de Berlín y Fitur de Madrid. Igualmente ha participado con monográficos especiales en las más importantes ferias inmobiliarias que se celebran en Gran Bretaña, concretamente en Manchester y Londres.

De todas ellas, es en la World Travel Market donde SUR in

English participa de forma más activa, pues desde 1987 tiene stand propio, aunque ya un año antes, concretamente en 1986, distribuyó un suplemento especial en la citada muestra en la que fue su primera experiencia internacional.

Por el stand de SUR in English en la WTM londinense han pasado los últimos cuatro ministros de Turismo que ha tenido nuestro país, Abel Caballero, Juan José Barrionuevo, Claudio Aranzadi y Javier Gómez Navarro, así como el consejero de Economía y Hacienda de la Junta, Jaime Montaner, directores generales, consejeros de diversas comunidades autónomas, el ministro de Turismo de Argentina, el embajador de España en Gran Bretaña y otras importantes personalidades, quienes han elogiado públicamente el papel desarrollado por el periódico en esta feria, con números monográficos sobre Andalucía, la Costa del Sol y Málaga.

10 YEARS OF SUR in English
Portada del suplemento especial de SUR in English con motivo de su X aniversario

Right: Cutting yet another Anniversary cake, with Pedro Luis, 15 years this time.

Below right: Liz Parry and I at a cocktail in the 80s.

Below left: Gerry, myself and restaurateur Garry Waite at the launch of *The Sunday Sun*, a paper which didn't stay the course - 21st February 1993.

Main: *SUR in English* 10th Anniversary event at the Bil-Bil in Benalmadina.

sunbathing topless at the luxurious Hotel Byblos. It turned out to be one of the greatest paparazzi *heists* in Spanish gossip column history. However, in order to protect HRH's honour, *¡Hola!* magazine bought the series of photos of the princess, never intending to publish them or let them even see the light of day. The publishers allegedly paid a monumental £1,000,000 for the privilege of protecting Diana's honour.

So overwhelmed was the Princess by the press interest in her stay on the coast that the National Tourist Board of Spain sent her flowers and a letter of apology. Meanwhile, in *SUR in English*, Joan in her own sweet way, published a very attractive picture of Princess Di - complete with bikini - and was given the assurance of the staff at the hotel that HRH had been, "courteous and lovely" as was to be expected.

SUR in English cumple 15 años con una tirada de 60.000 ejemplares

Se consolida como el primer periódico en lengua inglesa en Europa continental

SUR MÁLAGA

El lunes día 19 SUR in English celebró su XV aniversario. Esta edición semanal de SUR en inglés, con una tirada de 60.000 ejemplares, llega a su aniversario con los objetivos cumplidos y convertido en el periódico en lengua inglesa de mayo difusión de toda la Europa continental.

Portada del SUR in English

Cuando a finales de 1983 surgió el proyecto de hacer un periódico en inglés, nadie podía imaginarse que la idea se convertiría en un gran éxito tres lustros después. Hasta aquel entonces, en la Costa del Sol habían proliferado periódicos que nunca superaron unas audiencias mínimas y pronto desaparecieron e incluso en la mayoría de los diarios locales, en épocas diversas, se había puesto de moda editar una o dos páginas con noticias en inglés, que ni satisfacían a los ingleses ni a los lectores habituales. La experiencia, pues, no tenía precedentes, salvo en Palma de Mallorca. Lo que sí se sabía es que una amplia colonia de habla inglesa estaba necesitada de un vehículo de comunicación y que si se acertaba en el producto, éste podía tener futuro.

El futuro de aquel proyecto, que salió a la calle por primera vez en la tercera semana de julio de 1984, es hoy una gran realidad: SUR in English, edición en inglés –que no suplemento– de SUR que se distribuye todos los viernes, ha alcanzado los 60.000 ejemplares de tirada –regulada por OJD (Oficina de Justificación de la Difusión)–, con una audiencia media estimada de 270.000 personas. Su campo de influencia, que abarca toda Andalucía y Levante, Gibraltar, Melilla, Ceuta, Madrid y Barcelona, lo ha convertido en apenas tres lustros en el periódico en lengua inglesa de mayor difusión en la Europa continental.

Hoy en día, SUR in English cuenta con una plantilla perfilada, en la que Liz Parry, que entró a formar parte de esta publicación en 1985, y Eva Browne, que lo hizo en 1991, forman parte fundamental. Justo es recordar la labor realizada por Gerry y Joan Davies, artífices de SUR in English en sus comienzos, y fundamentales durante muchos años hasta el fallecimiento de Gerry Davies. Joan sigue colaborando habitualmente y sus recetas de cocina se han hecho famosas en la Costa del Sol. La plantilla actual se completa con Kate Rayner, redactora-traductora; Teresa Canales, administrativa de Publicidad; David Andrews, administrativo de Publicidad, y los colaboradores Rachel Haynes y Vivion O'Kelly.

Acercar a la colonia angloparlante al hábitat en el que vive y conectarla con la sociedad que le rodea, además de informar y orientar al turista ocasional, han sido los objetivos claros de esta publicación, que además realiza una amplia labor de promoción de la Costa del Sol y de Andalucía en las más importantes ferias de turismo e inmobiliarias del mundo, destacando la World Travel Market de Londres y la ITB de Berlín. Los objetivos planteados hace ahora 15 años han quedado ampliamente cumplidos. El gran reto de SUR in English, que también cuenta con edición en Internet, es ampliar su campo de difusión por toda Cataluña.

SUR in English

Happy 15 Year Anniversary

Circulation of 60,000 Copies a Week

The Leading English Newspaper in Continental Europe

When the idea of an English newspaper came up in 1984, nobody could imagine that fifteen years on it would be such a big success. Until then, there had only been a few attempts at English papers with minimal readerships and which soon fell by the wayside. Some Spanish newspapers included a few pages in English, which neither satisfied the foreign community nor the habitual readers. There were no precedents, but the growing colony of English speakers meant there was a need for a weekly publication, and the right format would have a good future.

The project, which materialised in the third week of July 1984, is now a lasting reality. *SUR in English*, the English edition - not a supplement of the *Diario SUR* - and which comes out weekly on Fridays, has reached a circulation of 60,000 copies, as verified by the OJD, (*Oficina de Justificación de la Difusión*), with an average weekly readership of some 270,000 people. The newspaper's area of influence is Andalusia, the East coast of Spain, Gibraltar, Melilla, Ceuta, Madrid and Barcelona, making it the English newspaper with the highest circulation in continental Europe.

Today the *SUR in English* has a dedicated team of its own; editor Liz Parry, who joined in 1985, and Eve Browne in 1991, are key players. And it is important to recognise the invaluable work of Gerry and Joan Davies, the creators of *SUR in English*, and whose efforts were vital for many years until Gerry's untimely death. Joan continues to contribute her recipes, which have become legendary on the Costa del Sol. The team is completed with Kate Rayner, Teresa Canales, David Andrews and contributors Vivion O'Kelly and Rachel Haynes.

Bringing the English speaking community closer to the environment it lives in and connecting it with the surrounding society, as well as informing the visiting tourists have been the clear objectives of this publication, which also does an excellent job of promoting the Costa del Sol and Andalusia at the most important tourism and real estate fairs in the world, especially the World Travel Market in London and the ITB in Berlin. The goals set out 15 years ago have been well and truly surpassed.

Opposite: Original article published in *Diario SUR* - 28th July 1999.

Fallece en Marbella Gerry Davies, uno de los pioneros de la Prensa en inglés en la Costa

MALAGA■ Gerry Davies, uno de los pioneros de la Prensa en lengua inglesa para los residentes extranjeros en la Costa del Sol, falleció ayer en Marbella a consecuencia de una grave enfermedad. Casado con Joan Davies, Gerry Davies vivió durante gran parte de su vida en la urbanización Calahonda, en Mijas Costa, siendo una persona muy conocida en todos los ámbitos turísticos y periodísticos de nuestra provincia.

Creador de numerosas publicaciones en inglés, fue uno de los inspiradores de SUR in English, experiencia que sin su trabajo y el de su esposa, no hubiese salido nunca adelante. Su idea de realizar un periódico distinto, que no compitiera con los periódicos extranjeros que llegaban a la Costa, fue un completo éxito.

SUR in English, de su mano, se convirtió en un gran fenómeno periodístico, para llegar a ser lo que es hoy: el periódico en lengua inglesa de mayor tirada y circulación de cuantos existen en España y uno de los primeros de Europa.

Gerry y Joan Davies formaron pareja no sólo matrimonial, sino profesional, porque ambos desarrollaron siempre juntos su trabajo, complementándose al máximo, formando un tándem que alcanzó su mayor éxito precisamente con la edición en inglés de SUR.

Gerald Davies Evans, natural de Llanythre (País de Gales) que llevaba 30 años en la Costa del Sol, su «tierra adoptiva», murió acompañado de su esposa en el Hospital de Marbella, a los 63 años de edad, y su entierro tendrá lugar mañana, sábado, a las 12 horas, en el antiguo cementerio de la citada localidad. Gerry contará siempre con el recuerdo de sus compañeros de SUR y de SUR in English.

Gerry y Joan Davies, en la fiesta del X aniversario de SUR in English

¿Qué traes hoy, Gerry?

PEDRO LUIS GOMEZ ■

¿Qué traes hoy, Gerry? La pregunta se repetía machaconamente todos los miércoles y los jueves cuando llegabas a SUR con tus pequeñas gafas colgando y con la máquina de escribir portátil. Venga, vamos a ver qué hacemos, decías en seguida, sin perder un minuto. 30 años llevabas en la Costa, Gerry, 30 años, y todavía te costaba hablar bien el castellano. Ese acento galés inconfundible. ¿Te acuerdas de la tarta que compartimos con motivo del quinto aniversario de SUR in English? ¿Recuerdas la fiesta del X aniversario? ¿Y cuando me hablaste de la organización de la fiesta del XV aniversario? Querido Gerry, han sido once años de trabajo juntos; once años y ni tú ni yo conseguimos nuestros objetivos: ni tú aprendiste bien el castellano ni yo el inglés. Gerry, por la redacción de SUR aún queda tu recuerdo, y nunca se irá. Tu letra ilegible aparece en algunos papeles; tus mensajes telefónicos, tus consejos, tus machaconas peticiones... Te vamos a echar de menos. Un abrazo fuerte, para ti y para tu mujer, que siempre formará contigo la pareja perfecta. Descansa en paz, Gerry.

Goodbye to Dear Gerry

It was not so long after this, in 1995, that sadly, 11 years into the adventure of *SUR in English*, Gerry Davies died, and although Joan continued to contribute her recipes and social column to the paper, week in, week out, it was never quite the same without Gerry.

But while the glitz and the glamour were gone, Joan and Gerry's contribution to expat life and the consolidation of the foreign resident's favourite English newspaper will be forever written in the annals of the Costa del Sol's curious and compelling history.

A Tribute to Gerry Davies

Pedro Luis Gomez

9th June 1995 in *Diario SUR*

"What have you got for us today Gerry?" This is the question that was asked repeatedly, every Thursday when you came to our office, with your glasses hanging off your nose, carrying the portable typewriter. "Come on now, let's see what we are going to do," you would say, without wasting a minute.

30 years you lived on the coast Gerry, and you still struggled to speak Spanish - your Welsh accent was unmistakeable. Do you remember the cake we shared on the 5th anniversary of the newspaper and the 10th anniversary party? And when you talked to me about plans for the 15th anniversary?

Dear Gerry, we worked together 11 years; 11 years and neither of us achieved our goal... in your case, to speak better Spanish and for me to learn some English...

Gerry, here in the offices of *SUR*, your memory is with us and always will be. Your illegible writing appears from time to time on bits of paper, along with your scribbled telephone messages and the echoes of your advice and your insistent requests.

We are going to miss you. A big hug for you and your wife; you always made the ideal couple, and always will.

Rest in peace Gerry.

Opposite: Obituary for Gerry in *Diario SUR* translated above.

PART 5

My Musings on Life

The Sounds of Spain

The Spanish, in general, are a volatile but polite nationality. They speak loudly and fast, expressing themselves without inhibitions. A bar or cafe in Spain is a mixture of sounds; the background disco music, the demands of the impatient customer, the profuse apologies of the patient but distraught waiter, the children laughing or crying and the ever present cackle of voices getting louder as consumption of wine or brandy increases.

Some years ago at the *vendimia,* the grape harvest in Jerez de la Frontera, the event was dedicated to Scotland. The town band was in large and loud evidence. There was, at the same time, flamenco music blaring from a loudspeaker and a lonely piper was struggling in vain to play his bagpipes. It was a disastrous cacophony of sounds, but nobody seemed to mind.

One of the most pleasing sounds is that of the fishing boats 'put-putting' away in the early dawn, and better still is their return with a healthy, abundant catch, in the cool of the evening. In the morning, there are the market sounds, the shunting of bikes, cars and trucks, the hooting, the blasting of horns and the hustle and bustle of the market with the stall-holders vying for customers, shouting out the best buy of the day, "*¡Calamares! ¡Boquerones! ¡Sardinas!*" and so on, to whet the appetite of the housewife. The eyes, the fins, the heart of the lettuce, the melon, all have to be examined and prodded before the final ritual of bargaining and buying, a slow but patient process.

Betwixt and between the market sounds are the cries of the lottery seller. The fishmonger and the baker woo this man, the one who has it in his power to sell the winning number. Are they going to win this week and be able to buy a fishing fleet or a supermarket? Or will they have to carry on listening patiently yet lovingly to the prattle of the housewives exchanging local gossip?

The goatherd, and he still exists, takes his goats to the milking 'parlour' be it in the centre of town or alongside the many new blocks of apartments. He calls each goat by name to be milked, '*Golondrina*', '*Naranja*', and speaks affectionately to each one while the housewives queue up with their churns. This is one sound that is going to be lost with the rapid growth of the high-rise blocks.

And so the evening sounds begin. The clinking of the glasses for the early evening cocktails, the popping of corks, the crickets as the sun goes down. Tired workers toot impatiently in traffic hold-ups. Flamenco music and hand clapping begin, and the discos are ready to open their doors. The shrill chirping of the *cicadas* and the deep throaty sounds of the bullfrogs are the sounds that belong to Spain.

Published as an article in an early copy of SUR in English, 1984.

Join The Club; Expat Life in Spain

Every day, people sell their homes and move on to better themselves, to be nearer their families or to start a new job. But it is not every day that you move to a new country of your choice. It is a big upheaval for everyone, a new life, a new place to live, a new school, a new language, new friends and maybe an exciting new venture. For reasons of their own, more folk are leaving the UK, heading for the sun and a better way of life.

Those who come to Spain have quite often holidayed here a few times and know the score, but it is still a gamble. Perhaps the kids won't like it - what about the language? The expat scene has changed considerably over the years. The serious ones are younger, they have a profession or trade, or just want to find work whatever it is to provide for their families and make an honest living. Lounging in the sun sounds like heaven, but after a few days, enough is enough. It's time to sort things out; the holiday is over.

First on the list is finding a good school for the children where they can mix with the locals, either a local Spanish school or, an international school, if they can stretch to the fees. While this is going on, father scans *SUR in English* to find a job. In boom time, there are plenty of jobs around, but these days, there are not so many situations vacant in the press. But then you can do what the Spaniards do, ask around. This is the main avenue for finding work in Spain.

Families tend to stick together until they get to know other people and mix in with the community. The schools help to do this; mums usually take the kids to school, both mother and child feeling apprehensive at first. Naturally, the mothers chat, and in no time at all, friendships are made which last until they move on. The mums meet for coffee and families get together at each other's homes. The children integrate well and pick up the language very quickly.

Over the years, dozens of international clubs and associations have started up on the Costa del Sol and further inland. Most have a strong membership list. For example, the Royal British Legion has about ten thriving branches up and down the Coast, where ex-servicemen and women attend weekly meetings. They arrange shopping trips to Gibraltar, outings to places like the Sierra Nevada ski resort or the Alhambra in Granada, and cultural sightseeing trips to Seville, Cordoba and Madrid. The trips are well organized and well attended. The weekly meetings of the Mijas Costa branch are bursting at the seams. There are several branches of the Lions and Rotary Clubs and a few Masonic Lodges who all do great work for charity. Others include Conservatives Abroad who frequently bring interesting guest speakers.

The British Society in Benalmadena is one of the stalwarts, and there are six branches of the American Club along the Coast. The Royal Air Force Club, is also in Benalmadena,

Friends of the Theatre in Fuengirola meet every few weeks, and so it goes on. For those who follow cricket, the Malaga Cricket Club is where many keen and dedicated players frequent. Bowls is popular with men and women, and with a competitive annual league, there are many good bowling greens along the coast, such as Santa Maria in Elviria, Miraflores in Mijas Costa and the Aloha Club in Nueva Andalusia.

Published as an article in SUR in English, 1995.

A Romantic Train Ride

The road from San Pedro to Ronda is a twisting highway with breathtaking views of sea and mountain, but the driver is usually too preoccupied by the hairpin bends to appreciate them. As an alternative, why not park the car in Algeciras and take the train to Ronda? You will be free to enjoy the panoramas of the countryside. The quaint, two-carriage train huffs and puffs its way around Los Barrios, San Roque, through the cork woods to Castellar and Jimena with spectacular views of both places. Such names as Gaucin, Cortes de la Frontera, Estacion Benoajan, Montejaque and La Indiana are fascinating, yet unfamiliar to many foreign residents on the Costa del Sol.

There are thirteen stops on route between the two towns. It is a steady climb by train to Ronda, and those who do not like heights will enjoy the journey far more than driving around those scary bends! This is a great bull-breeding area, and you may be fortunate enough to see the horsemen rounding up the bulls. They use a long pole that keeps the bull at arm's length! You may also spot some of the many storks in the region, nestling on the rooftops, while egrets and flamingos are a common sight. The area around Ronda is a paradise for ornithologists.

The railway line was constructed by British firm, Henderson Administration Co. Ltd in 1902, headed up by philanthropist, Sir Alexander Henderson, who later became Lord Farringdon, a title bestowed on him by Edward VII. He stayed in the area until the railway line was completed and enjoyed the experience so much that he felt inspired to build two hotels; the Reina Cristina in Algeciras and the Reina Victoria in Ronda.

Both of these stately hotels have, over the years, catered for Spanish and British aristocracies as well as international personalities. The Reina Cristina stayed open throughout the Spanish Civil War, and the Second World War, and it is said that many spies lived in the hotel during the latter. It is also famous as the Conference of Algeciras in 1905, at which representatives of Morocco, Spain, France, Germany, the United States, Great Britain, Italy and Russia divided Morocco into zones, each protected by Spain and France. The British journalist covering this conference was none other than a young Winston Churchill.

The visitor's book at the hotel reads like the *Who's Who*, with the signatures of King Alfonso XIII, Queen Elizabeth of Belgium, Queen Maria Jose of Italy, Lord and Lady Mountbatten, Charles de Gaulle, Juan Belmonte, Ava Gardner and a host of other luminaries. The Reina Victoria in Ronda resembles a Somerset Maugham-style country home. The grounds have trees and shrubs with an English country feel; even having primroses and daffodils growing in the gardens. And it is exciting looking down over the valley, over the famous Tajo, the Ronda gorge. It is fantastic scenery, and reminds me of North Wales.

Article published in the first edition of SUR in English, 20th July 1984.

Above: Beach side pool and the iconic pier stretching out into the sea at the famous Marbella Club Hotel.

Falling for Marbella's Charms

Everyone has heard of Marbella, now a world-class tourist resort. When we first drove there in the 60s, I thought it was just an ordinary small town, in a good position, but nothing to shout about. There are no great monuments, no splendid arches to go through (only one of the brash marble ones erected in the 90s by the outlandish Mayor Jesus Gil y Gil) and no particularly memorable ancient ruins to visit, only a few Moorish and Roman vestiges in the Old Town. Disappointed perhaps? Don't be. Marbella is different. Marbella is captivating; it has a charm of its own, which is utterly delightful.

My opinion of Marbella changed when I discovered the Old Town, with its pretty cottages and narrow, winding white streets creeping uphill and flowers blooming everywhere. I fell in love with it straight away. Who wouldn't?

Gradually we got to know Marbella and several people who lived there. Gerry and I used to drive down in the evening for a quiet drink at the Marbella Club, the legendary hotel started in the 50s by Prince Alfonso Hohenlohe at his fabulous beachfront *finca*. His cousin, Count Rudi von Schoenberg, was the main figurehead - and still is today. He has always been the consummate host and makes everyone feel welcome. Over the years, I got to know Count Rudi a little, along with his lovely wife, Princess Marie-Louise of Prussia; they have been part of the Marbella scene forever.

The Marbella Club Hotel became exclusive in the nicest possible way; the clientele included heads of state, royalty, well-known people in the film industry and a host of distinguished folk from all over the world. Enjoying a glass or two of wine, or a tipple of champagne *al fresco* in the bougainvillaea-strewn patios of the hotel will always linger in my memory.

The Marbella Club itself is delightful. A classic, inviting and alluring environment; a place you could stay forever. Most of the guests have frequented the hotel for many years and love the uniquely elegant atmosphere.

There always has been a certain glamour and mystique to Marbella which acts as a magnet for celebrities. When we first arrived, there were only a few key haunts, such as La Notte, where hostess Menchu always had some recent gossip for me! Here you would find Spanish celebrities, such as Lola Flores - matriarch of the Spanish flamenco dynasty, or Julio Iglesias. He could often be seen at Antonio's restaurant in Puerto Banus, another favourite with the celebs.

Dazzling Puerto Banus

Puerto Banus is another story. I remember being dazzled on my first visit many years ago. The spectacular leisure port, now populated with super yachts, designer stores and millions of tourists a year, was officially opened in May 1970 in a lavish ceremony attended by a host of stars including film director Roman Polanski, *Playboy* founder Hugh Hefner and guests of honour, Prince Rainier and Princess Grace of Monaco.

The then young Julio Iglesias was hired to sing for the 1,700 guests at the glittering inauguration. After such an auspicious start, Puerto Banus quickly became a favourite with the jet-set and, going hand in hand with this popularity, businesses were soon vying to set up there.

In those early days, visits to the port, one of the favourite haunts in Marbella, meant rubbing shoulders with the likes of Sean Connery and wife Micheline, Frank Bruno, Engelbert Humperdink, Tommy Steele, Jackie Stewart, Romy Schneider or singer Toni Dalli. The stars also liked to dine at Toni's famous pasta pavilion on the Golden Mile, as they did at the ornate Villa Tiberio, another glamorous Italian restaurant run by Sandro Morelli also on Marbella's famous stretch.

Feasting in Andalusia

Andalusia, southern Spain is a vast region with a variety of magnificent scenery, from the highest snow-capped *sierras* above Granada to the golden beaches of the Costa del Sol on the shores of the Mediterranean. With literally millions of visitors a year, the legendary climate and lifestyle act like magnets, beckoning people from colder climes to enjoy the year-round sunshine, warm temperatures and celebrated customs and *fiestas*.

The food and eating style in Andalusia are also great attractions; the natural foods and resources in Spain are abundant. Olives and almond trees grow profusely in Andalusia. The vast olive groves supply the rivers of olive oil that constitute a key ingredient in Spanish dishes and Mediterranean cuisine, replacing butter and other fats. A typical breakfast in Andalusia is fresh bread, toasted, a slice or two of tomato, and maybe a smattering of garlic, all drizzled with olive oil. Delicious and nutritious, this peasant's dish is fast becoming a favourite with the foreign residents too.

Lunch is the main event, the key meal of the day, eaten at leisure with the family and savoured. Traditionally three courses, starting with soup or a salad, followed by a fish or meat main course, the meal is finished off with fruit.

Fish is usually eaten at lunchtime, grilled or barbecued; sardines, and fresh anchovies caught in the Mediterranean are the most popular, alongside squid, baby octopus, tuna, swordfish, white fish and shellfish of all kinds, many of which are caught in the nearby Atlantic, in the Cadiz area. Halibut and turbot, as well as fresh salmon and *dorada*, are more recent and welcome arrivals. The fish market in any town is a sight to see and is usually bustling with housewives seeking out the most succulent catch of the day. You will no doubt see fish you have never set eyes on before. The same goes for seafood; fish stands look more like marine biology labs with every crustacean imaginable, from mussels and cockles, prawns of all shapes and sizes, to razor clams, barnacles and spiky sea urchins.

As for *paella*, the Spanish dish, *por excelencia*, blending the best of Spanish fish, seafood, Mediterranean vegetables, plump *paella* rice and saffron into a tasty, succulent and satisfying dish, it is traditionally eaten at lunch time; only the tourists order *paella* at night. As far as Spaniards are concerned, it is too heavy to dine on. *Paella* is typically the focus of a leisurely meal on a Sunday, cooked outside, usually by the men of the household.

Everyone knows what *tapas* are. The Spanish penchant for sharing small portions of many tasty dishes has become an international food sensation. Cooking *tapas* has become an art; serving up delicious little portions of fish, meat, shellfish, cheese and cured *jamón*, they are best savoured with a chilled beer, wine or sherry to whet your appetite for the meal to come. However, *tapas* eaten copiously make a good meal in themselves. It can be a case of trial and error, but the *tapas* habit makes you more eager to try new foods.

Food in Spain is a very visual commodity with vast tracts of land devoted to undulating rice fields, olive trees, orange and lemon groves, avocado plantations and hectares of vineyards, bulging with fat grapes. The fertile soil is perfect for cultivating sugar cane, tomatoes, figs, peaches, melons and strawberries. Everywhere you go, you can see the rich produce of the countryside and many villages in the hills have orange and lemon trees lining their roads. Then there are the spices; saffron, nutmeg, black pepper and paprika while the popular garlic mayonnaise, *alioli,* is said to have existed in Spain as long ago as 1024.

And let's not forget about *gazpacho*, the chilled soup made from pureed tomatoes, cucumber, garlic, onion, fine breadcrumbs, peppers, vinegar, salt and plenty of garlic. Originally a peasant dish, taken into the olive groves to stave off the hunger as the workers toiled under the fierce Andalusian sun, it has become a staple in the repertoires of Spanish homes and restaurants the world over.

The further south you travel in Spain, the more the eating habits change. Time is not strictly adhered to, unless it is a formal occasion, and meal times are a moveable feast. There are many days in the year when people eat *al fresco*, in the patio, on the terrace, in the garden or at a favourite *chiringuito* or beach bar.

International Cuisine

International cuisine is a much-used label, but what exactly does it mean? In my view it is basically a style or manner of cooking using the best ingredients peculiar to the country of origin, while borrowing ideas and trends from different cuisines around the world. It has a certain snob appeal to the gourmet.

Spain leads the world in the production of saffron, and it is often known as 'red gold' as it is the most expensive spice in the world. The caviar industry is controlled by Russia and Iran, and the best is only served at the tables of the rich. Now there is a rival, in the form of a high quality Spanish caviar farmed at Rio Frio in Granada.

However, we all have our favourite dishes, and they do not have to be expensive. One of the most memorable meals I have ever had in Spain was at a small *venta* in the mountains north of Madrid. We were served wild boar with homemade bread in front of a huge log fire. The worst meal we ever had was in a hotel on the Welsh border where there were flies in the soup and the hotel manager was too busy having his own lunch to attend to us (*Fawlty Towers'* style).

When travelling in Europe, I have always tried to seek out the *bistros*, the *trattorias*, the inns, the *auberges* and enjoy the typical meals of the day; delicious platefuls of good home cooking. The Planahaus in Weisbaden, where father brought back pheasant and fish from his hunting trips in the nearby Taunus, was a great favourite, washed down with sturdy steins of frothy beer.

Once Gerry and I drove from Spain to Trieste in Italy on a trip and decided to cross into what was then Yugoslavia, to have a look around. We had gone from pesetas to francs to lira to dinar. No euros in those days... With all the zeros on the bank notes, some currencies gave the illusion that everything was very expensive. On the contrary, it was so cheap. One meal; in a cosy workman's cafe, was a tasty stew made with herbs and spices.

The mention of Austria, particularly Innsbruck, reminds me of a delicious blue trout I once ate there. And also the rich cream pastries. Although pasta is not my favourite dish, I was served some genuinely delicious minestrone soup served in the *trattorias* of Rome.

As Lord Lytton wrote,

> "He may live without love - what is passion but pining?
>
> But where is the man who can live without dining?"

Garlic Galore

Like it or leave it, garlic has become a standard ingredient in the preparation of food in both southern and northern Europe. Most people who cook with garlic use the Spanish variety to flavour their dishes as it's the most widely exported.

Both Chinese and Egyptian garlic are the stronger, followed by Argentinean, whilst the native bulbs from France, Italy and Spain come way down the list in strength. It is said that a Chinese clove of garlic is 12 times stronger than a Spanish one.

To retain the flavour, connoisseurs recommend not using a crusher. This apparently destroys the allicin, which is a sulphurous compound and gives it a metallic taste. The strength of the garlic is determined by the amount of allicin, and this is also what gives the bulb its health properties. The way to get the best out of your garlic cloves is to chop them finely like most Spanish and Italian cooks do.

Always add the garlic towards the end of cooking time, and remember, the smaller the clove, the stronger the taste. Many people love garlic, others have a love-hate relationship with it. A friend called Alice detested the taste and smell of garlic; little did she realize she has no doubt eaten it many times quite unwittingly.

The Chocolate Craze

Why is it that the world and his wife adore chocolate? I admit, I have been fascinated myself by the catalogues of a chocolate company I recently discovered. They made me see chocolate in a totally new light. To the uninitiated, chocolate was either plain or milk, with or without fruit and nuts. I was in for an education...

This chocolate company made up a clever brochure all about the subject, complete with illustrations to make your mouth water. Pure sophistication. The founders of this magical company had funded large projects to improve cocoa farms in Ghana, bettering the lives of the locals and in so doing, the quality of the raw ingredients too.

They absolutely refuse to tolerate such unpleasant ingredients such as hydrogenated vegetable fat or artificial colours in any of their products. "Good chocolate is a natural, wholesome thing and we plan to keep it that way", they proclaim. Fighting talk! They go on to talk about being committed and ethical. Committed, for sure; you only have to go through their product catalogue to see that they are masters at this work. It has style, good design and a wonderful presentation to entice the public.

I worked my way through the list of delicious names drooling over the comforting truffles with alcohol and real cream, and the amaretto almonds; to die for, but I did wonder a little about the wisdom of chocolate dipped bacon...

Man About The Kitchen

Does your husband or partner take an interest in cooking? Nowadays, more and more men folk are taking over the household duties, sharing the shopping, the preparation and cooking of the evening meal. Why not? No longer is domesticity the domain of a woman; there are plenty of non-*macho* tasks involved in homemaking. When it comes to cooking, many men love it! To some, after a day at the office, cooking a meal is a kind of therapy, an opportunity to wind down. "What shall I cook for dinner tonight?" is now the question on many a man's lips.

It begins as a kind of joke, "Of course I can cook!" Then it becomes fun and a challenge. You could give my husband Gerry a cookery book and he would peruse it for hours. "How about this? Do you fancy that?" He was an imaginative and inventive cook, but everything had to be weighed out carefully before he started. Gerry also needed an assistant to fetch and carry. "Where is the saffron? How much salt should I put in? What pan shall I use?" He also needed someone to keep his glass topped up!

Nowadays, there are all sorts of kitchen accessories for chaps, like cookery diaries, plastic aprons decorated with his favourite red Ferrari or glamorous pin-up, tankards to put on the kitchen dresser as well as innumerable cookery books and so it goes on. Your birthday and Christmas present problem is easily solved.

So the meal is ready, delicious I must say, and most rewarding for the cook. But then what happens? My chap would retire to watch TV, with his glass nicely filled. The aftermath in the kitchen was not a pretty sight. I still don't understand how anyone could use all those pots and pans. "That's your department," I would be told. There must be an answer to that somewhere.

So much for a *man* in the kitchen...

PART 6

Life On My Own

Going it Alone

Throughout their married life, couples tend to share the duties. More than likely, women work to contribute to the household expenses, look after the children, do the shopping... Life is good, comfortable. Everything in the house is working - carefully looked after by the spouse. The duties are divided; you take care of one side, your partner, the other - it's automatic. But what happens when you lose your beloved spouse, and you are torn apart? When there is no husband to look after you, then what? Your life is shattered. You are on your own.

Eventually, you are down to basics, the bulb in the bathroom goes, you shop and buy a replacement, but can you put it in the socket? Can you reach? Your husband always did it. You relied on him totally. Now you are in control of the car. How much petrol do you put in it? There are so many tasks the man of the house generally takes care of; I'd never even opened a bottle of wine myself until Gerry died and even using a screwdriver was a novelty for me.

So now you are a person on your own. When you ask someone, not a friend, to fix a plug or build a shelf, you are prepared to pay for it, no doubt about that. You decide to go to people you know, but if you are a woman on your own, you are overcharged, automatically. They think you are stupid or ignorant, and that you don't know any better.

Perhaps when someone comes to fix a plug, they get a bit anxious, chatting more than usual and accepting a coffee or a beer. They think you want their company but actually you just want the job over and done with. Is it a *macho* thing? They are pleased with themselves, smug even, and go back to their lives, duty over.

In the first instance, your friends surround and comfort you all say the same kind words; "Remember we are here for you Joan, whenever you want something, ring and we'll be there". OK. So you do ring a few times, but then you stop. "Why?" you ask yourself. The answer is obvious.

Downsizing My Life

Moving from a house to an apartment is a big step. Our house in Calahonda was high on a hill, with glorious views over the Mediterranean and the Sierras of Andalusia. It was a happy house and I loved it. Friends would say the property had a warm and homely feel, and I believed it had. From the moment we viewed the house, I didn't want to see another; and I lived there with Gerry for many happy years. However, the time had now come. My husband had died nearly ten years previously and all of a sudden I realised,

Right: My good friend Herta Fritz takes me along as co-pilot for the Mini Club Marbella day in 2007.

Below: More recently, outside my apartment in Mijas Costa.

everything around our home seemed to look sad and neglected. It was as if the walls understood all I was thinking. The doors needed a lick of paint, the pool needed grouting and the garden was a mess. I saw the ominous beginnings of rising damp and felt helpless and despondent. "Snap out of it girl!" I said to myself. I do tend to talk to myself when I'm down! "Do something positive, quit moping." Big decisions had to be made; the house was too big for little old me to cope with and reluctantly I had no choice but to downsize. It was time to sell. I finally put the house on the market knowing deep down that it was the right time to move on.

The word had got out that "Joan is selling her house". Then the questions came, "Where will you live?" Are you going home - back to the UK? This is my home. After forty happy years in Spain, the thought of moving away has never entered my head; regardless of my roots, my life is here.

I put the house in the hands of several capable agents. I had never sold a house on my own before and the thought was rather daunting. I was a complete novice at selling. Unlike my sister who had changed houses frequently. I found that there was more to it than her blasé advice would suggest; "Keep to your price and don't budge. Leave everything to the agents, it's their job."

The agents visited the house and took down all the details; the size of the plot, number of bedrooms, etc. Then I signed the permission for them to sell the property on my behalf - that was step one. "I've done it now", I thought. "I can't change my mind - there is no going back now." On to step two: get the house shipshape. A little cosmetic treatment was needed; moving furniture, de-cluttering, buying flowers for the table. I waited for the phone to ring, and waited. The flowers were wilting already. Everyday I did a quick flick with the duster.

The first call from an agent had me in a mild state of trepidation. "Can I bring the couple up now to see the house?" Suddenly I had misgivings. "Do I really want to sell?" Yes, I do I said to myself. "They are on their way to the airport," the agent said. I wondered, "If they are going to the airport, then they must have seen other places and I'm last on their list." They arrived, had a quick look round, looked at their watches and said, "Thank you very much," and left. "So this is what I could expect, is it?" I thought. They weren't in the house for more than ten minutes. I felt very put out.

There is a scale of potential house buyers; some who are just curious and want to pass the time until they have to go to the airport; those who can't afford it and will put in a low bid, hoping that you're desperate to sell, and those that say: "We might as well have a look at the property while we are here." Then there are those that are genuinely interested. It is a process we, as vendors, all have to go through; no matter how time consuming, frustrating, even boring... You learn how to deal with it through experience. You start to recognise those nosy browsers, the people who just want to tell their friends

Above: Painting of Gerry and I as a young couple, entitled "Hope". Painted by an African American artist, Edward 'Eddy' Webster who came to live in Fuengirola having retired from his work in the US postal service in New York. He passed away in Malaga in 1977.

they have been looking at property in Spain... You take a careful look around to make sure everything is in order and open the door. Hundreds of questions go through your head and you make the number one mistake, offering them a cup of tea.

One day, an agent arranged a viewing of the house on behalf of a couple from Hong Kong which sounded promising. They were a professional couple and had come to the Coast to look for a property. They were youngish, but had decided to retire early and come to a sunny climate. "It seems so big and spacious to us," they said. "In Hong Kong, apartments are all high-rise and have very little floor space. The city is so highly populated," They were rapturous about the upstairs terrace, saying, "This is as big as our whole apartment!" I offered them tea and coffee, and answered all their questions. "How far are the beach and the shops?" and that sort of thing...

The couple from the East were really interested. They asked, "Will you go back home when you sell?" "No, Spain will always be my home", I explained. On leaving, they looked at each other and said, "We'll have to go back to Hong Kong and arrange for our things to be shipped, but this is ideal." I was excited; I finally had a sale on my hands.

Then reality hit; where would I live now? Where did I want to go? I knew what I wanted; a two-bedroom, two-bathroom apartment on the first floor, preferably with a fairly large sitting room, small kitchen, terrace, the usual communal pool and gardens, and good security. My new home needed to be convenient for shops and not too far from the sea. Surely it's not too difficult to find the perfect little place? That's what I thought, and that's where I was wrong.

Never in my whole life had I bought a property on my own, making all the decisions myself. And it was perfectly obvious to every agent I met. Every apartment I saw was lovely, and I told them so, but they were never quite sure what I was looking for. I was shown dozens of apartments, all with a similar formula and layout, but couldn't make up my mind. Frustration and impatience began to show. Thankfully, an old friend appeared on the scene and guided me to the beautiful apartment which I have lived in since.

It takes time to acquaint oneself with new surroundings, especially when the home is smaller. Lots of things needed to be done, but that is part of the excitement and drama of moving. My first plan was to fit a new kitchen. I made the living area open plan with the kitchen in cream. It's a large and airy lounge with French windows leading on to a sunny terrace. Next I bought some big, bright cushions for my large cream sofas. My small collection of art adorns the living room walls, sailing paintings, a watercolour of the Snowdon mountain railway (page 140) and a similar one of the Cairns-Kuranda railway, (page 152) on which I travelled while visiting Australia.

Another painting is a portrait of Gerry and myself standing on the waters edge, looking up at a rainbow and is simply called *Hope*. I love to have familiar things around me. It feels like home here, but I still haven't unpacked all the boxes; big house to a much smaller apartment... I have too many clothes, too many possessions and far too much clutter. I find it difficult to be ruthless, but every now and then, I go through things, fill a couple of rubbish bags and throw them out or have them taken to the charity shops.

There are many advantages to living in an apartment; I like the thought that people are around me, not with me, but in the same building. It is comforting, especially after living in a detached house on my own, often without any neighbours, for ten years.

I also like sounds, other people's chatter, movement, and the footsteps of other people going out to work in the mornings; the neighbours are generally very considerate and helpful. When I go on holiday now, it's nice to think, I can just go away, lock the door and enjoy myself. It's a good life.

My Mornings

I enjoy getting up early when there's nobody around, listening to the many sounds the dawn brings; the animals, birds, bees, the doves in the cork oaks. I start the day in good form, always with a fresh cup of coffee on the terrace. I always feel like the rest of world is waking up with me... If you wake up early, say at 7.30am, you are ready for the day. I don't need company in the mornings, the sounds of the nature are enough. Then I prepare my breakfast - usually toast, marmalade and some fruit, or a Spanish *tostada* with tomatoes and olive oil - a good healthy start to the day.

On the long, balmy summer evenings, I enjoy looking at the stars in the sky until the early hours.

Broken Confidence

Three years ago, when I was 81, I sneezed and unbelievably broke two ribs. I was hospitalized for a few weeks and then returned home, but osteoporosis had set in and I had great difficulty in walking. My brother Alun came to look after me and slowly I began to recover. I managed to start walking again with the aid of a stick. I had lost my confidence completely at first, but slowly I have managed to regain it, and now, sometimes I forget to use my stick, even when I go out.

Where there's a will, there's a way.

Above: Lunch with my dear friends Karina and Oriel who was at school with Gerry at Llandovery College in west Wales.

Left: With my sister Brenda at the Parador in Malaga.

Below: A family wedding with all the finery. Left to right: Lowrie, Jenny, Alun, me, Brenda Sian, Ken and James.

Above: Johnny, John Carter, James, Lowrie, Lara, Jonathan, Jenny, me, Brenda , Sian and extrended family.

Above Left: With my sisters Sian and Lowrie, nephew Johnny and former Prime Minister John Major in 2001.

Above: With lifelong friend from Wales, Elenna O'Harry.

Left: Annabel and Mary Jones, friends for 30 years, a visit in 2008.

Below: The Hughes girls! With sisters, Sian, Jenny and Lowrie. Shropshire late 1980s.

Above: Dinner with the Costa Press Club with
members Adrian Bracken, Karen McMahon,
Jesper Pederson, Paul O'Connell, Jack
Nusbaum, Chris Chaplow and novelist
Rod Younger.

Right: With Herta Fritz and Josephine Quintero.

Below: A healthy turnout for the Costa Press Club
at the Hotel El Fuerte in Marbella in 2012.

Joining The Costa Press Posse

With so many different foreign language publications servicing the needs of the large expatriate communities on the Costa del Sol, it was just a matter of time before the idea of a press club for foreign journalists would spring up.

As one of the 'pioneers' of the Coast's publishing scene for expatriates, it figured that I would also be involved with the creation of what is now the well-established Costa Press Club. The seed of the idea was planted during a press event held by the Mijas Foreigner's Department. I was sitting with Jesper Pederson, Liz Parry, Suzan Davenport and Gillaine Hathaway and we were discussing what a great idea a Press Club would be, to network, share information and support visiting journalists from overseas.

As to be expected in Spain, the association took a while to gel and be formally crystallized into a non-profit organization, complete with reams of complex paperwork - which Jesper and Peter Leonard handled. The attendance at each meeting has to be hand written in a special Log Book. My name certainly crops up plenty of times! The first official meeting took place on 27th May 2004 at the Puente Romano Hotel in Marbella.

I have been an active member since the Costa Press Club began, attending as many meetings as I can. The meetings are monthly, and always over dinner or *tapas*, with a speaker talking about something relevant to the Coast's press people. I have always enjoyed getting together with my various press friends and colleagues, meeting visiting journalists and catching up on local news and gossip!

When the club was started, I was still writing my Facts & Faces and Food for Thought weekly columns in *Sur in English*, and so I was active in organizing the meetings to take place at various new venues and restaurants. I would sometimes write up the meetings in my events column. Being on my own, the Costa Press Club has been a big part of my social life in recent years.

Joan Davies, pioneer of English media in Spain, receives Communicator Award

David Baird, author of 'Between Two Fires', and Chris Chaplow of Andalucia.com took home awards in non-fiction and website categories

SUR IN ENGLISH

This summer it will be 25 years since Joan Davies, together with her late husband Gerry and the Spanish firm Prensa Malagueña, publishers of SUR, started SUR in English. It was fitting therefore, that this year Joan received a special Honorary Communicator Award from the Costa Press Club.

This is the third consecutive year that the club has presented its Communicator Awards to members of the foreign press for their outstanding contributions in different fields.

Joan has been living in Spain since 1964 and has had numerous articles about Spain published in England, Scotland and Wales. While working Madrid in 1966, she became accredited by the Club Internacional de Prensa for the Daily Express.

Presenting the award to Joan, Jesper Sander Pedersen, president of the Costa Press Club, said, "You are a role model and an example to follow for every journalist living and working in the southern part of Spain. You give us the confidence and inspiration to write another article and convert another good idea into something real."

Spanish history

The winner of the Communicator Award 2009 in the category of non-fiction is David Baird, author of the book "Between Two Fires - Guerrilla War in the Spanish Sierras". Based on more than five years of research and personal interviews, the book tells the fascinating story of the Maquis, the

WINNERS. David Baird (l), Joan Davies and Chris Chaplow (r) with Jesper S. Pedersen. / VINCENT DE VRIES

post Spanish Civil War resistance movement, and gives readers a convincing, detailed picture of a little-known period in modern Spanish history.

The winner of the Communicator Award 2009 in the websites category is Chris Chaplow, founder and managing director of Andalucia.com, one of the leading websites offering up to date information about the southern Spanish region. The first version of Andalucia.com in English was started in 1996 and the Spanish version was launched in 2006.

Held on Thursday March 12th at El Fogón restaurant in La Cala de Mijas, the awards dinner was attended by members of the press club and invited guests.

The Costa Press Club is an international association and forum for foreign journalists and media representatives living and working on the Costa del Sol. It currently has 50 members from eight different countries, and holds monthly meetings and dinners.

My good friends Jack Nusbaum, Herta Fritz and Gillaine Hathaway usually attend. I've got Jack to thank for saving my life a few months ago when he stopped me from choking on an olive at one of the events! Jesper and Herta very kindly ferry me back and forth by car; my racing days are sadly over!

In 2004, the Club made me Honorary President, which I was thrilled about! In the same year, I also won the Communicator of the Year award. Jesper says that I am considered a 'role model' in how to create a foreign language publication, although, of course, I'm sure that things would be very different if we tried to launch a newspaper now!

The club has done really well; over 100 members of the press attended the 10th anniversary celebrations in June 2012. I was pictured with UK publicist Max Clifford, who was guest of honour and speaker at the event.

SETTING. THE EVENT WAS HELD AT THE BEAUTIFUL VINCCI SELECCIÓN ESTRELLA DEL MAR'S BEACH CLUB.

Left: Press cutting from the Costa Press Club's 10th Anniversary at the Hotel Vincci del Mar Beach Club where publicist Max Clifford was a guest speaker. June 2012.

JOAN DAVIES WITH MAX CLIFFORD.

SUZAN DAVENPORT, MARY HARBOE AND LIZ PARRY.

KATE RAYNER, ASH BOLTON AND JOSEPHINE QUINTERO

UWE SCHEELE AND HERTA FRITZ

ANNE BOWLES, GILLAINE HATHAWAY AND JACK NUSBAUM

Gala event to celebrate Costa Press Club's tenth anniversary

The Costa Press Club, whose international membership is made up of editors, journalists, freelance writers, publicists and photographers working in southern Spain, celebrated its tenth anniversary with a gala dinner at the Estrella del Mar Beach Club last week.

The guest speaker was Max Clifford, who entertained more than 70 club members and friends with off-the-record anecdotes about his experience as one of the world's best known publicists, and afterwards took questions from guests.

The Costa Press Club holds monthly meetings at various locations on the coast, and acts as a voice for foreign journalists resident in Spain. For details go to www.costapressclub.com

MAX CLIFFORD WITH CPC PRESIDENT JESPER SANDER PEDERSEN

Photos: **SUR in English and Adrian Bracken**
More photos of the event **www.surinenglish.com**

Below: Another of my favourite paintings of the railways in Snowdon, Wales.

Honouring My Welsh Roots

Here I am in Spain - a country I love yet I am still nostalgic about Wales. I have fond memories that will never be erased from my heart. The choir, the festivals, the music, the people, the small villages - you are always welcomed by the Welsh folk - I love Wales! I'm a sentimental person, my eyes even well up when I hear a brass band. I will always have a sense of nostalgia about Wales, the country where I was brought up and went to school. I cry at the drop of a hat.

For my sins, I can also lay claim to starting the Welsh Roots Club on the Costa del Sol. This is a very informal club and again involves a monthly social gathering, this time around lunch - usually at the Streets of London pub in Mijas Costa or Bogarts in Calahonda. We started the club in the late 90s; Peter Roberts now runs Welsh Roots having taken over from Delyth Bressington, Gethin Jones, and Howard John before him.

Many of our members are great singers - particularly the men who frequently belong to Welsh choirs, and this certainly livens up proceedings. My good friend Wyn Calvin, a hugely popular Welsh entertainer, has performed in choirs here. Some of the members speak Welsh - and it is good fun to get the opportunity to brush up on my Welsh from time to time. Attendance varies, but the Welsh are generally a good fun, spirited bunch, and enjoy meeting new faces.

St. David's Day on the 1st March is a big day for us, when we celebrate the day of our Patron Saint. As this is a key date for us Welsh expats, whatever function we organize is normally well supported by local Welsh residents and plenty of Welsh tourists holidaying on the Coast at the time. On St. David's day, all Welsh people try to make an effort to celebrate the special day with traditional food, song and prose for those not inhibited by the sound of their own voices. Quite often a local male choir will be drafted in. Numbers have reached up to 70 people, all ready to paint the town red, white and green. For a long time I was the heart of the club, calling up all the members and getting them together. This is definitely one of my fortes!

In Fine Welsh Voice

The South Wales Male Choir, one of the largest male choirs in Britain performed twice at Salon Varietes in Fuengirola back in February 1984. The choir of 80 voices earned a roof raising, rapturous applause, after both of their two fantastic concerts.

The grand finale of their concert tour was on St. David's Day at the John Mackintosh Hall in Gibraltar in the presence of the Governor, His Excellency, Sir Francis Richards and his wife, Lady Richards. The Governor announced that they greatly appreciated such a fine festival of joyous song and laughter. Welsh singing star, Sian Hopkins and the choir's president, Wyn Calvin MBE, affectionately known as the 'Welsh Prince of Laughter', attended all the concerts.

Recently the choir visited Hungary, Prague and Poland. Previous tours included America, Singapore, Canada, Holland, Belgium and France. The choir has also had the honour of singing before Her Majesty the Queen, Heads of State and once performed for President Nelson Mandela who was welcomed to Cardiff Castle. They have appeared before royal patron, HRH the Prince of Wales on several occasions who refers to them fondly as 'my choir'. An accomplished group of performers, they have wowed audiences in venues from the Sydney Opera House and the Hollywood Bowl, to London's Royal Albert Hall. Imagine what a privilege it was for the people of the Costa del Sol to enjoy them live in a small and friendly venue in Fuengirola.

Wyn Calvin MBE - The Welsh Prince of Laughter

I have known Wyn for many years and I cherish both his friendship and that of his lovely wife, Carol. They live in Cardiff, so I only see them on occasions when they visit the Coast - which is never often enough for my liking. He has a voice to die for, as is the expression, and I could listen to him all day. It is a deep, resonant voice and he uses it to perfection.

The Calvins have been very helpful and loving to me over the years, and I admire them tremendously. Wyn has been in show business for over 60 years. He is Wales's premier Pantomime Dame - one of the best in Great Britain. In 1991 he became the first Welshman ever to be elected 'King Rat' of the Grand Order of Water Rats, the show business fraternity and charity. Honoured with an MBE for his services to charity in 1989, Wyn has been the Welsh chairman of the Variety Club of Great Britain, and has done much to help handicapped and deprived children. He is a Freeman of the City of London, a Fellow of the Royal Welsh College of Music and Drama, and a Member of the Welsh Lively Guild.

A champion after-dinner speaker too; there is no finer gentleman than Wyn Calvin. He is my much loved and admired friend.

Left: With my good friend Wyn Calvin MBE, singers Sian Hopkins and Ivor Emmanuel; best known for his role in the film Zulu, and Luigi Rabaiotti in Marbella.

Below: Entertainer, Wyn Calvin MBE with ladies in Welsh dress after a show at the Salon Varietes in Fuengirola.

Haughty Portmeirion

The venue for my nephew Paul's wedding was the exclusive Hotel Portmeirion. I knew it well, having been brought up in the area, but had never stayed there. Clough Williams Ellis, an eccentric aristocrat, opened the Hotel in the 20s. As a child, I remember him strutting around in his breeches and sports jacket. There were whispers from the local people, who worked in the kitchens and gardens, of princes, members of the Royal Family, famous film stars who stayed there, but it was all very discreet.

The hotel has always welcomed a celebrated clientele from its beginnings, many from the literary world; George Bernard Shaw, HG Wells, Bertrand Russell and Noel Coward. The latter writing *Blythe Spirit* there in 1941. World famous architect, Frank Lloyd Wright stayed there in 1956 and, in 1966, Portmeirion Hotel was discovered by Patrick McGoohan, who used it as the setting for his classic TV series, *The Prisoner*.

The scenery in this part of Wales is magnificent; Snowdon is a dramatic backdrop, particularly when the peak has a light dusting of snow. Situated alongside the wide estuary of the River Dwyryd where it flows into Cardigan Bay, Portmeirion Hotel is not overly grand, or smart. From the outside, it looks just like an ordinary, well looked-after hotel in a beautiful, natural setting. It has comfort, simplicity, an air of haughtiness and its own inimitable style that shrieks exclusivity. The weddings are held in Hercules Hall, which was built to house a unique barrel-vaulted 17th century sculpture ceiling. The Portmeirion is always popular - the *in* place; that is, if you can get in... Paul and his wife had to wait two years for their big day after making their reservation.

Left: My father, John Trevor Hughes in Pwllheli. c.1980.

Below: Me with Lowrie and Colin's children, Jessica and Jonathan.

PART 7

Joan's Travelogue

The Trip of A Lifetime

In 2002 I took the trip of a lifetime. My sister Lowrie planned a trip for us to visit our sister Janet in Australia, do some sightseeing in New Zealand, and return via America.

I fell in love with Australia and that incredible feeling of space. We did a lot of sailing as my nephew, cousin Iona's son Richard, who has won dozens of sailing prizes, took us out on his yacht. Although small and nimble, a slight chap, Richard sails solo all over the world.

Our journey started in Melbourne, where the family greeted us. We so enjoyed seeing everyone again. The city has a large population of over 3 million and prides itself on its sports. Home to cricket in Australia many of the world famous test matches take place at the Melbourne Cricket Ground in Yarra Park. We spent a day or two viewing the main sights, the Eureka Tower, the city centre, the Rod Laver Arena - the scene of many top tennis tournaments, and then it was time to set off and view some of the most beautiful sights in the world, starting in Sydney.

The Wonders of Sydney

After many tears, kisses and heaps of affection, we left the family and with great anticipation headed off to see Sydney. Our first stop was of course, the iconic Sydney Opera House, one of the world's great waterfront destinations. It's a fascinating building, which I thoroughly enjoyed visiting, except for the 200 steps! We strolled along Bennelong Walk, which encompasses the Opera House and Bennelong Point, a place of great significance in Aboriginal history.

Next we went to Darling Harbour, which, in the 1900s, grew into the colony's busiest commercial port with wharfs, markets, mills, and wool storage sheds. Today it's a fabulous area to visit, replete with good restaurants and gift stores, as well as an Aboriginal Art and Culture Centre. The Powerhouse Museum, also in the harbour, is one of Sydney's key cultural attractions, having been running under various names for 125 years and boasting 400,000 artefacts on show.

We took a long trip around the harbour in a luxury catamaran, saw Sydney Harbour bridge and watched the breathtaking views glide before us from the comfort of a spacious foredeck. The National Maritime Museum shows how the sea has shaped Australian history and culture, and Sydney Aquarium is one of the most spectacular in the world.

Last but not least, we visited the harbour side Fudge Shop home of delicious toffee, chocolate and fudge in all colours and flavours including exotic mango, paw-paw and passion fruit. We watched the owner prepare toffee on a big table in the shop. He spread out the sweet smelling goo with a long-handled brush and once it was cool he broke it into bite-sized pieces with a hammer and offered it to the visitors to taste. His marketing worked - we bought several boxes!

The Great Barrier Reef

We left Sydney in New South Wales for the coast of Queensland. The flight touched down at Townsville, and from there we went on to the island of Hayman, which forms one of the Whitsunday group of islands located on the Great Barrier Reef. A small seaplane transported our party, Lowrie, my niece and nephew and myself to Hayman.

From above, the first thing that hit me was the dazzling colours. The blues range from the indigo of the deep water to the turquoise and aquamarine of the shallower sandy reaches. In sharp contrast, the thick forest-clad hillsides stand out in their lush, deep greens and yellows. Rocky outcrops of volcanic boulders dot the islands and at the waterline where the reefs and beaches resemble strings of white pearls. Below the surface of the water the fish and coral reefs can be seen creating beautiful shapes and patterns.

The pilot was a friendly fellow and he pointed out places on the other small islands as we flew over them before we landed in the grounds of the Hayman Island Resort, one of the Leading Hotels of the World. It was here that we a stayed of five glorious days. I was fascinated to be in this incredible place, so far from home and I couldn't wait to explore!

The outer reefs form part of the vast Great Barrier Reef, a few miles to the east of Whitsunday Islands. Aboriginal people would travel among these enclaves to forage for seasonal foods. They were skilled seafarers and made canoes and fishing gear to suit the conditions. The Whitsunday Islands are a collection of continental islands off the central coast of Queensland. They were named after Captain James Cook's journey in 1770 when he passed through the waters, now known as Whitsunday Passage. However, the term is a misnomer; because of an error in time keeping, it was actually Whit-Monday.

I remember it was terribly hot when we were there; hats are a must 'down under'. I still hold with affection the straw hat I bought, and although it holds wonderful memories, it is somewhat battered now.

Today the area is the most popular yachting destination in the Southern Hemisphere, the harbours are full of tourists looking for fun; the yachts, cruisers and the shops, bars and restaurants are alive with the buzz of people. The Whitsunday Islands are a true paradise of immense natural beauty, and quite unforgettable.

The Cairns to Kuranda Railway

One of my favourite paintings is a keepsake from the stunningly beautiful trip we took on the Cairns-Kuranda scenic railway. The picture depicts the steam train as it passes at soaring heights over the breathtaking Stony Creek Waterfalls. The famous Cairns-Kuranda Railway was a mammoth feat of engineering, opened up to passenger travel way back in 1891.

The search for a route from the Tablelands to the coast was the task of Christie Palmerston, an expert bushman and pioneer. He apparently wrote a note saying: "No chance of track, 20 days without rations, living on roots principally." However, he persisted and did eventually mark out a few routes and a decision was made that would shape the future of Queensland. The Barron alley gorge route was chosen, and the people of Cairns were jubilant. This line was a total of 75 kilometres. The construction and working conditions in the swamps and bush were bad, and they had little equipment. At one time, 1,500 men, mainly French and Italian were working there.

We had gone to the village of Kuranda on the Skyrail Rainforest Cableway and we were to return on this line, the Scenic Railway to Cairns. We boarded the shining red train carriage, one of 12, pulled by an immaculate red and black steam engine. We climbed to an altitude of 327 metres, and the train snaked through countless tunnels, around interminable curves and over many seemingly precarious bridges, high above hair-raising gorges and breathtaking waterfalls. We eventually came down through the sugar cane fields to Cairns. It was the most exhilarating journey I've ever experienced.

The painting I bought to remind me of the experience of that epic train journey as it as it passes the Stony Creeks Waterfalls was by Alex Reardon. I cherish that painting to this day - it hangs in my apartment, alongside a picture of Snowdon, which is close to my childhood home in Wales. Both works of art have pride of place in my home and I love them dearly.

Above: Painting of the Cairns-Kuranda railway at the Stony Creek Bridge in Australia. This windy,
21 mile route travels through 5 long tunnels and climbs around 985 feet.

The Fresh Taste of New Zealand

The next leg of our journey was to Auckland, New Zealand, where we stayed at the Hyatt Regency Hotel for five nights. It was at the top end of the city, in a green area near the University. There is a Sky Tower in the centre of Auckland that dominates the skyline. This tower and entertainment complex have stunning views over the city - known as the City of Sails. Viaduct Harbour, a historic area, was once home to the fishing fleets, but rather like Sydney, it was given a new lease of life in the year 2000 as the Sailing Village to the America's Cup.

From Auckland we travelled out to Rotarua, one of the tourist centres of New Zealand. It sits on the edge of the North Island Volcanic Plateau and the area is sizzling with thermal activity. The first was Rainbow Springs where we enjoyed a guided walk through the beautiful flora and fauna display located beside a large natural water spring, home of thousands of rainbow trout. We then headed off to the Kiwi House to view New Zealand's famous bird.

Our next stop was an agricultural show at Rainbow Farm. Other coaches had arrived with more tourists. There was a hand show of nationalities and it turned out we were the only Europeans in the audience, just the four of us! The sheepdog handler, preparing to show off his skills introduced his dogs. "You'll never see dogs like these anywhere else in the world!" he proudly proclaimed. "We have them in Wales and Scotland." I shouted bravely, "And we have rugger players too!" I added in *sotto* voice.

The best part of the tour was yet to come. We travelled around Rotorua's lakeside area alongside the geothermal steam pools, famous for their therapeutic qualities, towards the Maori Arts and Crafts Institute of Whakarewarewa. Here we were greeted by the local Maori where we obliged by taking part in the tradition of *Hongi*, pressing of noses, and greeting everyone with the welcome, *Kiarora*. We were shown beautiful Maori carvings, flax garment making as well as a life-size replica of a traditional Maori village. We braved the geo-thermal area, past boiling mud pools and the famous Pohutu Geyser, which spurts out boiling water 20 times a day; the powerful gushes reaching 100 feet into the deep blue skies.

The sights and sounds of New Zealand were wondrous. We were shown the fascinating caves of Waitomo famous for its glow-worms. Unique to New Zealand, these industrious creatures drop sticky threads, which incredibly, light up, luring insects into their trap. We were mesmerized by the beautiful spectacle.

New Zealand offers such a cornucopia of exotic experiences.

Meeting Cousin Iona

One of the highlights of my trip to the Southern Hemisphere came towards the end of the journey. I have a first cousin called Iona who, many years ago, went to live on outskirts of Auckland, with her husband. I had not seen her since we were in our teens, but we were very close at the time.

Much like myself, Iona spent most of her childhood in Wales. Later, she went to college in London, and I went to Bangor; we lost touch with each other at that point. I heard on the family grapevine, she later taught in Bristol, where she met and married an army officer. He was attached to the Gurkha regiment and they spent many years abroad. I never dreamt that our paths would cross again, however, when I received the itinerary for our trip, I made a point of finding out her address through mutual cousins.

I phoned Iona, and arranged to meet her the following day in the lobby of our hotel, the Hyatt Regency. I was so excited...

"How will we recognize each other?" we both wondered. Promptly at three o'clock, I walked into the crowded reception, feeling a little lost. Suddenly from behind me, I heard my name,

"Joan!"

"Iona?" I said,

"How did you recognize me?"

"You're exactly like your mother!"

There was no answer to that!

It was a strange feeling, meeting up with a close relative on the other side of the world. We greeted each other warmly: I was happy, yet at the same time, overwhelmed, and I know that she felt the same.

Tony was waiting in the car outside, we walked arm in arm to meet him. He was a large amiable man with twinkling eyes. He gave me a welcoming bear hug. "We'll take you for a run out to see some of the countryside, then we'll head home."

We drove through Cornwall Park, a perfectly groomed wooded area within the city itself, full of exotic native trees. Next was the volcanic summit of One Tree Hill, also known as Maungakiekie, which offers spectacular views over Auckland. Our drive took us past Eden Park, the grounds famous in New Zealand for All Blacks rugby in the winter and international cricket during the summer. We passed more key sporting locations; a couple of horse racetracks and the Hampton Downs motor racing track.

Finally we reached their home: a long, low, single storey house, high up on the outskirts of Auckland, surrounded by manicured green lawns. Inside, apart from the two decks (we call them verandas) it was a similar to a home in rural England, comfortable and cosy, with chintzy sofas and chairs.

Shortly before dinner, Iona's daughter Deborah and husband Keith arrived, with their son Richard, who had broken off his journey from Wellington to Singapore, where he lives with his family. They had all come to meet me.

After a few gin and tonics, we sat down to dinner, a chicken casserole, flavoured with delicate spices. This was followed by a delicious apple and mascarpone sponge pudding. I enjoyed the subtle flavours of the 'Kiwi' cuisine; with its Asian influences. Tony served his own special house wine and it was an evening to remember. I shall never forget the warmth and the welcome I received from my cousins on the other side of the world.

Our Whistle-Stop US Tour

Two Ladies in Las Vegas

Las Vegas means 'the plains' or 'the valleys' in Spanish. Located in the south-western part of the state of Nevada, USA, at one time the whole area was a swamp full of wild vegetation. In 1829, a Mexican trader called Antonio Armijo was leading a posse of horsemen along the Spanish trail when he decided to deviate from his normal route; it was then that he discovered this lovely oasis in the middle of the desert. Sometime later, Mormons followed him there from Salt Lake City. The initial growth of Las Vegas can be traced to 1931 when the Nevada legislature formally legalized gambling. In the ensuing years, the increase and popularity of the casinos and gambling saloons boomed. It is unique, a city that has to be seen to be believed, and this is why my sister Sian and I had chosen to visit, to see it for ourselves. We arrived at our hotel in the late afternoon, hot and bewildered. The temperature was 104 degrees Fahrenheit. Neither of us could speak, and my first words evoked the conflict of emotions; shock, trepidation, then excitement. "What on earth were we doing here?"

We looked at each other and smiled weakly. "Let's check in and have a drink". The check-in area was the size of a ballroom, and we joined a queue of large and extra-large travellers who seemed to know where they were going. We didn't. Even our voices seemed to dry up. As soon as we spoke the response was, "Gee, where are you guys from? We love your accent!"

Sian and I loved the Bellagio shopping promenade, overlooking an artificial lake. Every half an hour it comes to life with a mesmerizing ballet of water fountains, beautifully choreographed to music. We walked through the Casino Royale, a vast gambling area with more than 2,500 slot machines; black jack, roulette, mini-baccarat tables and poker.

It's the entertainment capital of the world, so every evening, after dinner, we went off to seek out something different. Having just missed Celine Dion and Sir Elton John we tried to get tickets to the Tom Jones show during his last two days in town, but sadly it was fully booked.

Eventually we discovered a great little bar with live music groups. We went there on several nights, listened to the bands, chatted and people watched. It was fascinating. We had to remind ourselves that we were in the centre of an American desert. One evening a group of five girls came in wearing figure hugging designer jeans, shiny boots, minuscule jazzy tops and white Stetsons. They were young and strikingly beautiful. We later learned, they were from an American Indian tribe called Hualapai who live on the rim of the Grand Canyon not far from Vegas. The girls wanted to party and have fun. After their third Daiquiri, they joined the group on stage, singing and dancing. Then as quickly as they arrived, they disappeared into the night.

Chicago is for Shopping

Chicago, known as the Windy City, was pleasantly surprising. I found it intriguing; well laid out and immaculately clean. Sian and I visited the main attractions; the Essanay Studios, home of the Charlie Chaplin films, an antique mall and the famous skyscraper, Sears Tower. It was all great fun.

Importantly for us girls, Chicago is a shopper's dream; *"My Kind of Town"* as Frank Sinatra crooned... Sian and I stayed on Michigan Avenue, known as the Magnificent Mile. This is where you can find the famous stores: Bloomingdales, Saks 5th Avenue, Macy's and Tiffany & Co. However, we were told before we arrived that Marshall Fields was 'the only place to go'. One of the longest established department stores in the world, Marshall Fields is to Chicago what Harrods is to London. The store was built at the turn of the 20th century and is much more than just a place to shop.

It was built in five stages, in neo-classical style and opened in 1907. Said to be the second largest department store in the world, after Macy's in New York, it is a true emporium with courtyards, one of which is like an Italian palazzo, housing a striking Tiffany dome of mosaic glass and a fairytale fountain. There are two food courts, one on the 7th floor, and another in the basement. Frango Mint Chocolates are the specialty of Marshall Fields and with good reason. It's an 'awesome' place, as the locals say, and it's difficult to know where to start. Thankfully, a smart young shop assistant gave us a few tips. He suggested we 'tour' the city without leaving the building by simply following the 'Windows on Chicago' on the top floor. He also suggested a cocktail to accompany the glorious panoramas. It was all quite delightful! It makes me sad to think the Marshall Fields store is now part of retail history.

Pier 39, San Francisco

In San Francisco, a city that has always fascinated me, we booked two nights at the Sheraton on Fisherman's Wharf. Unlike the friendly Australians and New Zealanders, we found that the Americans were not so ready with their smiles. However, we found our way to Pier 39, one of the most popular shopping areas close to the Golden Gate Bridge; a tourist's dream location. As we approached, we could feel the upbeat mood; perfect for holidaymakers looking for souvenirs and those willing to spend their dollars on a good day out. It had all the hurly-burly of a fun fair, full of quirky shops, bars and fish restaurants. It all runs down to the waterfront where pelicans can be seen swooping and perching on the mooring posts. Sian suggested we had coffee at Dante's Seafood Grill overlooking the water's edge and afterwards, we succumbed to a little shopping.

I remember the jewellery, especially the silverware being quite original. Strolling to the end of the pier, we could see the former prison of Alcatraz, which sits exuding a sinister air in the bay. A much more pleasing sight was the seals resting on the timbered floats and moorings.

We wandered back to Dante's for lunch where we had already perused the menu. I can still remember the delicious, homemade crab cakes with honey and teriyaki sauce. Ambling back, we popped into various speciality shops for gifts. As they say, "Eat, shop, stop and walk." Sian and I certainly did all of that, and were royally entertained by colourful, talented street performers.

Like most large cities, there are a number of shopping centres on the outskirts. We visited The Cannery, in Monterrey, formerly the Del Monte plant, once the largest peach canning facility in the world. Saved from demolition in 1960, it was later transformed into magnificent mall it is today. The old courtyard was retained, together with olive trees, flowers and lush foliage. The Cannery is a unique building of winding walkways, balconies and bridges, many designer stores and award-winning restaurants.

The next morning, before our flight to Los Angeles, Sian had arranged for our taxi driver to give us a quick tour of San Francisco. He drove down Market Street; the centre of business and commerce and the wide avenues of Nob Hill and Telegraph Hill. We took in Union Square and the beautiful Ghirardelli Square with its fountains and landscaped gardens. Then the taxi wove its way through China Town, home to the largest Chinese community outside Asia. We headed down Lombard Street, said to be the most twisty road in the world; a short very steep hill with dozens of bends, bordered by magnificent villas. Lastly, we took a final look at the majestic Golden Gate Bridge where the Pacific sweeps into the San Francisco Bay; an impressive and quite unforgettable vista.

After many suggestions we decided on a trip to Warsaw and Cracow in Eastern Europe, a country completely unknown to us. Living in a warm climate, we were not really bothered about temperatures. It could be 25 degrees one day, said a seasoned traveller, and 15 the next. Anyway it shouldn't be cold.

We booked a ten day trip, flying to Warsaw, with a stop in Madrid, where we joined our three hour flight for the next part of the journey. During the Second World War the city of Warsaw was annihilated by the Germans. Historic relics and monuments of Polish culture were completely destroyed but not long afterwards, the impossible was achieved. A totally torn and battered city was rebuilt within a few years. Historic buildings in the Old Town and new streets were carefully reconstructed: the Royal Castle was rebuilt and new districts, wide streets and thoroughfares were made. There is still evidence of the old socialist regime, with its huge, ugly old blocks of concrete apartments and grey walls. The city is constantly expanding. Today Warsaw, a city reborn, stands proudly with its new skyscrapers, modern commercial buildings and shopping malls.

Elegant houses

We were booked into the Radisson SAS Hotel for three nights. It was late afternoon when we arrived, rather weary but excited. The weather did not look promising, grey and dull, but we were optimistic, what else can you be? The hotel was good, very comfortable and the restaurant served international cuisine, a blend of the different cultures in Europe. The next day we began to explore the city, armed with a map and booklets of information. It was quite a walk from hotel to the centre and we headed for the Old Town, reputed to be one of the most beautiful parts of Warsaw. The Market Square has been the centre of life in the city for centuries. It is lined with imposing, elegant houses belonging to the rich burghers and merchants who brought prosperity to this country. It is alive and humming with people selling their paintings, wooden dolls and beautiful carvings which they were doing, sitting down, totally oblivious of the passers-by: a fascinating sight.

Sound of music

The sound of music was never far away from the squares. Spain has the guitar and Poland has the accordion, both emitting a different type of music and both beautiful. Small groups of musicians, some in traditional dress and others in everyday wear, just trying to make a living moved from café to café. The monument of the Mermaid of Warsaw, restored after the war, stands again in the square as the emblem of the capital. There were many tourists walking around or riding in the horse-drawn cabs, having a tour of this wonderful city, with so many churches, monasteries, beautiful buildings and monuments. I was fascinated by the many children and school groups who were there with their teachers, no doubt having a history lesson about their beloved country, something they would never forget. It was far more interesting than I had imagined. It was incredible that this new Warsaw had emerged after such devastation. It is a "brave new world" brought into being by the courage, bravery and sheer determination of the people of Poland. It is a city marching into the future, becoming one of Europe's most exciting places. From world-class restaurants to space age shopping, it is today the buzzing capital of a lovely country. A little foot-weary after the sight-see-

A glimpse of Eastern Europe

JOAN DAVIES

Warsaw is constantly expanding and today it is a city reborn which stands proudly with its new skyscrapers, modern commercial buildings and shopping malls

WARSAW. View of the Old Market Square.

CRACOW. Wawel cathedral.

ing, we boarded a train for our three hour journey to Cracow

The train was very comfortable, but

there was no dining car: lunch was a cup of coffee, no charge, but on return we had to pay.

Cracow

We arrived in Cracow, known as the Royal City, the Polish Mecca, the day after Pope Benedict XVI left the city and shortly before the Football World Cup. John Paul II came to Cracow Cathedral after he became Pope in 1978. His first mass as Pope was in the crypt and there were photographs of him everywhere. Our hotel was the Holiday Inn, not far from the Market Square, one of the largest medieval squares in Europe. This has been the focal point of the city's public, religious and economic life, the place where everyone sits and watches the world go by. The Cloth Hall dominates the centre of the square. It is impressive both inside and out and houses small, compact vendors' stalls, full of handicraft - lace, souvenirs, jewellery particularly amber for which the area is famous, leather, silver and paintings. The weather was cold and wet so we spent some time here together with scores of children on an educational visit. We had a coffee in one of the many cafes surrounding the square where we met some fellow Brits. They were drinking vodka. "Try some, it will warm you up." It certainly did. They also recommended a cocktail, known as Zubrowska, which we got to appreciate. It was made up of a special brand of vodka called Bison, and apple juice, which became our regular pre-dinner drink. There were many superb restaurants in and around the square. One of our favourites was Wierzynek, which had an impressive list of distinguished guests - George Bush, Charles de Gaulle, Robert de Niro, Kim Philby, Yehudi Menuhin and their own Lech Walesa. There was an interesting story behind this. A few centuries ago, Nicholas Wierzynek invited royalty to this mansion to celebrate the wedding of the King's grand-daughter. He was then granted royal permission to receive the nobility and dignitaries, a custom which has continued to this day. Most of the top restaurants are below street level, probably in the servants' quarters or the huge wine cellars of the tall, elegant houses belonging to the rich merchants.

Traditional food

The food was mainly good, traditional old Polish cuisine. For centuries the kitchens of the Polish nobles had adapted French, Italian, Lithuanian and Jewish dishes, but the native favourites are cabbage, beetroot, apples and pears which grow abundantly on their own green and fertile land. A typical meal is a meat and sauerkraut stew known as Bigos, very rich and tasty on a chilly day. Most menus included duck and goose, always with apples. Then there is Kopytka which are potato dumplings, a basic food, but not for the figure-conscious. The desserts are quite delicious: apple fritters which are light as a feather; Babka, a honey-spice cake and a scrumptious cheesecake. The restaurants pride themselves on a good table and excellent service. The Polish people are courteous and friendly wherever you go. In Cracow, especially they are always smiling.

We returned to our hotel to find the scenario had changed: 29 Scotsmen had arrived for a stag jamboree! Thankfully they were a great bunch and we enjoyed their company. The next day, we saw them in their kilts, walking around the square, a fine sight for all to see. We did not see the house where Chopin was born, but there's always the next time.

East Side Story

After much consideration, I decided on a trip to Warsaw and Cracow in Eastern Europe Poland was a complete unknown. Living in a warm climate, I was not really bothered about temperatures. "It could be 25 degrees one day, and 15 the next," said a seasoned traveller. So I booked a 10-day trip, and flew to Warsaw.

During the Second World War, enemy bombers demolished most of the city. Historical relics of Polish culture were completely destroyed, but not long afterwards, the impossible was achieved. A totally torn and battered city was rebuilt within a few years. Historic buildings in the Old town and new streets were carefully reconstructed, including the royal castle and new districts with wide avenues. There is still evidence of the old Soviet regime, with its huge, ugly old blocks of concrete apartments and grey walls. The city is constantly expanding. Today, Warsaw, a city reborn, stands proudly with its new skyscrapers, modern commercial buildings and shopping malls. I stayed at the Radisson Hotel for three nights with a friend.

Armed with a map we explored the city's Old Town, the most beautiful part. The Market Square has been the centre of life for centuries. Lined with imposing elegant houses belonging to the rich merchants and burghers who brought the country prosperity. The square was alive and humming with people selling paintings, wooden dolls and artefacts. There were craftsmen in the square creating beautiful carvings, totally oblivious to passers-by.

The sound of music was never far away from the squares. Spain has the guitar, and Poland the accordion, both emitting a different type of music, equally beautiful. Small groups of musicians, some in traditional dress, trying to make a living, busked from cafe to cafe. The monument of Syrenka, the mermaid of Warsaw, restored after the War, stands proud in the square, an emblem of the capital. Tourists ambled around on foot, or riding in horse-drawn carriages, touring this wonderful city of churches, monasteries and striking monuments.

There were groups of local school children out with their teachers learning *in situ* about the history of their beloved country, which was possibly far more interesting than they imagined. Warsaw today is a brave new world brought into being by the courage and sheer determination of the people of Poland. Fast becoming one of Europe's most exciting places, it has everything from world-class restaurants to designer shopping; Warsaw is a buzzing metropolis.

The Polish 'Mecca'

A little weary after sightseeing on foot, we boarded a train for a three-hour journey to Cracow. The carriage was very comfortable, but there was no dining car: lunch was a cup of coffee.

Cracow, known as the Royal City is the Polish 'Mecca'. We arrived the day after Pope Benedict XVI had visited the city, and shortly before the Football World Cup. The previous Pope, John Paul II, had come to Cracow Cathedral after he was ordained in 1978. His first mass as Pope was in the crypt and there were photos of the momentous occasion all over the town.

Our hotel was not far from Market Square, one of the largest medieval *plazas* in Europe. This has always been the focus of the city's public, religious and economic life, and is the place where everyone sits and watches the world go by. The Cloth Hall dominates the centre of the square. Impressive both inside and out, it houses compact stalls laden with locally made handicrafts; leather and lace, jewellery, particularly silver and amber for which the area is famous.

As the weather was bitterly cold, we took refuge in one of the many cafes surrounding the square where we found ourselves chatting to some fellow Brits. They were drinking vodka, and suggested we try some, to warm us up. We did, and it certainly hit the spot! They also recommended a cocktail made from Bison, a special brand of vodka, blended with apple juice. Known as Zubrowska it became our regular, pre-dinner drink.

Home

To be there where the sea

Laps the stones on the shore

To be there where the buzzard

Will gracefully soar

To be there where the otter

The crow and geese

All live in a world

Completely at peace

Where the docks and the bays

Are caressed by the tide

And the sun mainly shines

On the rolling hillside

To be there on the hills

Where the wild goats roam

Where one could be happy

To call it home

-- o --

by Joan Davies & Bobby Kerrera